"Few professionals think of personal vulnerability as a characteristic they should work to develop. But in this book, Tom DeLong shows that only through vulnerability can you find the courage to make real change in your life and work—moving from doing the wrong things well to the way station of doing the right things poorly. This book is essential reading for anyone who wants to achieve personal and professional growth rather than just continue to muse about it."

—C. Allen Parker, Deputy Presiding Partner,
Cravath, Swaine & Moore LLP

"This book gives readers key questions they need to ask for self-reflection as they develop personal action plans in order to acquire new leadership behaviors. Tom DeLong gives a strong recommendation for creating a truth-speaking advisory network to help reduce anxiety and support personal growth. Finding the courage to take risks to change—one awkward step at a time until you get it right—is the first step to a renewal of self-worth as we forge a path to 'making a difference.'"

—Mary Graham Davis, Chair of the Board, Mount Holyoke
College, and President of Davis Consulting Group LLC

"Does the reality of your career match your innermost aspirations . . . or do you have a nagging sense that you may be stuck, marking time, or lacking true direction? With candid stories and compelling real-life examples, *Flying Without a Net* enables us to ask ourselves the tough questions—and provides the tools for mapping a course for change."

—Laura King, Global People Partner, Clifford Chance LLP

"Tom DeLong provides an insightful and practical assessment of factors that keep high-performance individuals from reaching their full potential. With his focus on the value of embracing change and the steps to address the anxiety that change can produce, he has created a valuable tool to help leaders and aspiring leaders excel."

—Ruth Porat, Chief Financial Officer, Morgan Stanley

"Are you striving for high performance, but are unsure about your career? *Flying Without a Net* will help you to deploy your talents and take your destiny into your own hands. It will provide you with advice on how to change, overcome your secret fears, and achieve more while living a fuller life."

—Daniel Vasella, MD, Chairman, Novartis AG

"Tom DeLong, a self-confessed, card-carrying 'high-need-for-achievement professional,' has written a useable, provocative, and highly readable book. In *Flying Without a Net* he provides a change process to overcome anxiety and traps that keep you from taking action."

—Tom Watson, cofounder, Vice Chairman Emeritus, Omnicom Group, and Dean, Omnicom University

FLYING

WITHOUT

A

NET

FLYING
WITHOUT
A
NET

Turn Fear of Change into Fuel for Success

THOMAS J. DeLONG

Harvard Business Review Press

Boston, Massachusetts

Library of Congress Cataloging-in-Publication Data

DeLong, Thomas.
    Flying without a net : turn fear of change into fuel for success / Thomas J. DeLong.
        p. cm.
    Includes bibliographical references.
    ISBN 978-1-4221-6229-3 (alk. paper)
    1. Employee motivation.   2. Achievement motivation.   3. Change (Psychology)
4. Job satisfaction.   5. Success.   6. Career development.   I. Title.
    HF5549.5.M63D454 2011
    658.3'14—dc22

                                                                    2010054392

The paper used in this publication meets the requirements of the American National
Standard for Permanence of Paper for Publications and Documents in Libraries and
Archives Z39.48–1992.

To Mildred and Joseph DeLong,
Mom and Dad

CONTENTS

Part 3
The Four Traps That Keep You from Change

Part 4
Getting Over It
Tools for Turning Fear of Change into Fuel for Success

Late one evening I sat on a bench in Grand Central Station in the early
'90s trying to figure out whether I had the energy or desire to jump on
a Metro North Train for the ride home. I reflected on whether I should
have ever moved our family from the Rocky Mountains to New York
to take on a job that felt bigger than any capabilities I imagined I had.
I fretted about whether it was possible to make the changes that my
boss wanted and the organization needed. I wondered whether I could
facilitate the senior management team in a way where they would work
together more effectively.

I also agonized over whether it was possible to open up the myriad
offices we planned to establish in the coming months. I wrestled with
whether it would ever be possible to get the traders and investment
bankers to support one another while they were in the same room or in
the same building. And I had serious doubts about whether I could give
the necessary feedback to the CEO so that I could help him improve on
his already high level of performance.

When I looked at my watch and realized that it was 10:00 p.m. and
that I had been sitting on the bench for two hours, I knew something
had to give. After I managed to lift myself off the bench, board the
train and head home, I began thinking about anxieties and traps that
plague *high-need-for-achievement professionals*, a group in which
I'm a card-carrying member. Ever since I finished my doctoral studies

in the winter of 1979, I have been contemplating this subject and how ambitious, driven people often are their own worst enemies. As a Harvard Business School professor and previously as an executive with Morgan Stanley, I have had countless opportunities to interact with and study high-need-for-achievement professionals.

High-need-for-achievement may be an unfamiliar term, but you know the type: driven, ambitious, goal-oriented, myopically focused on succeeding, and so on. Throughout this book, I'm going to be using this and other terms interchangeably to refer to the high-need-for-achievement type.

My interest in these professionals dovetailed with my consulting and writing related to the transformation process. As I listened and learned and tried to apply principles of change theory to situations involving achievement-craving professionals, I began to develop a change process for this group—a process that helps them learn and grow rather than stagnate.

For thirty years I've wrestled with how to help those who are either stuck on the bench at Grand Central Station or who perhaps should stop to consider life. This book is written with these individuals in mind. As you'll see, it's not a traditional "academic" book; it's not heavily footnoted or jammed with case histories and references to other scholarly works. Instead, it's usable, provocative, and (I hope) highly readable. As you might guess from the opening of this preface and in the personal stories I relate in coming chapters, it's the book I wish I had possessed when I began my journey. Given the times in which we live, I suspect it's a book that will be relevant to your concerns.

Today both individuals and organizations face threats from all sides. The volatile economy, the impact of new technologies, the changing shape and cultures of corporations, the increasing challenges facing families, the increased demands on our time and energy—all of these ratchet up everyone's anxieties. High-need-for-achievement professionals, though, react especially strongly to these threats. We become convinced that we've fallen out of favor with the boss, that our business will fail, that we'll be passed over for a promotion, that we'll be downsized out of a job, that we'll become B players when we always thought of ourselves as A players.

Given our uncertain and unpredictable environment, even the brightest among us are anxious. In response, we hunker down, blocking ourselves from new challenges. We become locked into our routines, focusing on tasks that we know we do well and ignoring challenges and opportunities that might stretch our capabilities. We know this response hurts us and our organizations. But we fear making ourselves even more vulnerable by committing mistakes while learning something new or testing a new approach.

Organizations are filled with smart, ambitious people who are less productive and satisfied than they should be. Doctors, lawyers, teachers, engineers, bankers, and business leaders and their managers find that they can't reach the goals they set or find the meaning they seek. Yet some of these high-drive professionals overcome their fears, adopt new behaviors, and lead enormously successful, fulfilled lives. Unfortunately, they are a minority.

What is going on? Why are the best and the brightest in all age groups and in all professions struggling like never before? Perhaps more significantly, what can you do about it if you're a high-need-for-achievement professional? How do you escape this malaise and become more effective, successful, and fulfilled?

You learn to fly without a net. In other words, you discover how to move through the anxieties that keep you from taking action; you begin to gradually trust your ability to learn, grow, and change and you realize that this ability will help you in your chosen profession. Flying without a net doesn't happen overnight. It's a process that begins with awareness of the forces that escalate your anxieties, act as traps, and cause you to turn to unproductive behaviors for relief. The process also involves adopting counterintuitive practices that give you the courage to *do the right things poorly* before doing the right things well. And it's a process that requires you to be vulnerable, something that driven professionals don't like to be. To achieve more and gain greater satisfaction from your work, though, you must be willing to open yourself up to new learning and experiences that may make you feel uncertain at best and incompetent at worst. These feelings are temporary and a prelude to a greater depth and breadth in your professional and personal life.

Let me tell you a bit about what you can expect from this book. First, you'll find many stories of high-need-for-achievement professionals like yourself. Some describe people who are trapped by their anxieties, and some are about individuals who avoid and escape these traps and change in highly productive ways. Second, you'll encounter a great deal of advice about what to do if you want to be less anxious and achieve more but are floundering—checklists, questions, and exercises. As a driven professional, one of your strengths is your task orientation, so these prescriptive elements should play to the way you live. Third, you'll find a framework that places all the book's advice and concepts in a compelling context. A few key graphics illustrate this framework and will provide guidance as you discover how to transcend your anxieties and find the courage to try new behaviors and change.

The book is divided into the following conceptual sections. In the first two chapters, I will establish the basic concepts for the book: chapter 1 defines high-need-for-achievement professionals and their particular traits and helps you determine where you fit within this category. Chapter 2 gives you the framework mentioned above and provides examples and information that will help you use it to your advantage. This chapter also makes the point that the desire to achieve at all costs may help people rise to a certain level in organizations, but will eventually place a ceiling on their achievement as well as their satisfaction.

Chapters 3 through 5 will make you aware of the basic anxieties that confront you and control your behaviors in negative ways. They will demonstrate that when you don't confront your anxieties, it is counterproductive on multiple levels. Each chapter deals with a particular cause of anxiety—lack of purpose, isolation, and feelings of insignificance—and how you can counteract their effects.

Chapters 6 through 9 outline the traps you may fall into as you respond to these different types of anxieties. Being busy, comparing, blaming others, and worrying are the ways we try to resolve and reduce our anxieties, yet in reality these responses only cause us more distress. That is the irony of change. The more we attempt to resolve our internal anxieties, the more we reinforce and feed them through counterproductive efforts.

Finally, chapters 10 through 14 introduce a group of tools that assist you in dealing effectively with your anxieties and their related traps so that you can allow yourself to be vulnerable, grow, and change. From self-reflection to agenda setting to creating a support system, these tools help break the vicious cycles that hinder our change efforts. You will learn the ways to drop your defenses and reach out in courageous and productive ways.

Let me give you a sense of what I hope this book will accomplish by sharing the comments of one high-need-for-achievement professional after a speech I gave. I was addressing a group of high school principals, and after the talk, one of them approached and thanked me. Then he said, "Professor DeLong, I'm forty-three years old, and I find my job frustrating and not enjoyable at all. There's little that makes me want to get to work in the morning. But the good news is that I only have twelve years until retirement." I didn't know how to reply. But now I do, and this book is it. I want him to understand that if he is going to be an effective leader who inspires and guides his students during a critical time of life, he needs to get past his fears and frustrations, his routines and rituals. Rather than get bogged down in his worries about the school board and media criticism, he needs to be more bold rather than more conservative, more willing to experiment rather than preserve the status quo, more open to fresh ideas and new educational technologies rather than adhering to fear and failure as motivations.

If he were able to do these things, not only would he be a better principal for his students but he would no longer hate getting up in the morning before school; he would relish the challenges and his courage in tackling them.

I had a number of people in mind besides this principal when I decided to write this book. Here is a partial list of these individuals; see if you're among them:

- For those who are paralyzed by their fears to the extent that they refuse to learn or try anything new.

- For those who appear successful by all external measures but feel flat, feel unmotivated, and feel like they are just enduring each day.

- For those who have given up and are waiting for something to happen to them rather than creating an action that moves them closer to their dreams.

- For those who are verbally abused by others for trying to change.

- For those who get in their own way when they need to change, creating barriers that are totally in their own minds rather than in their environments.

- For myself, since I wanted a concrete reminder that fear can get the best of me at times when I least expect it.

The old model for high-need-for-achievement personalities was invulnerability—being opaque, emotionally detached, risk averse, and coldly analytical. This book will make the case for a new, vulnerable model and offer direction for professionals who no longer know which way to turn.

And this book is for those who are stuck. If you feel as though you're falling behind and need a hand, this book will provide that hand. If you feel like you are not using your talents in significant ways, this book will give you options for doing meaningful work. If you find yourself disconnected from your field, your organization, your team, your significant other, or yourself, this book will suggest paths toward reconnecting.

If you're like many high-need-for-achievement professionals I know, you feel like it's been too long since you've had control over and freedom in your work life. You doubt whether your addictions to work and achievement could be managed.

I'm here to tell you that they can be managed, and that this book provides the information, inspiration, and process for doing so. I realize that at this point you have to take this statement on faith. But as one of the people interviewed for this book told me, "There are simply times when you have to have faith in yourself and others."

I'm asking you to have faith not just in your need to achieve but your ability to change.

With that thought in mind, let me introduce the next chapter . . . and you to yourself: the high-need-for-achievement professional.

PART I

WHY WE

FEAR

CHANGE

CHAPTER ONE

The Achilles Heel of the Driven, Ambitious Professional

DON THOMPSON COULD DO NO WRONG. When he joined a high-powered consulting firm right after receiving his MBA from a top school, he quickly demonstrated the qualities that would allow him to make partner in record time. Charming, smart, with business savvy, he not only was good with clients but was skilled at the work—he was especially adept at helping client companies reformulate their strategies. Within seven years he had earned a reputation that drew organizations to the firm seeking out Don's expertise. For twelve years, Don flourished. Then he hit a wall.

It wasn't that he suddenly became less charming or skilled than he had always been. He continued to do excellent work. But subtle signs began to appear that he was no longer the brightest star in the firmament. He was bypassed for membership on some committees that were charged with shaping the future of the firm. When the firm began courting a major prospective client, Don wasn't included in the process. The senior partners didn't invite him to lunch at their clubs as often as they once had.

This was driven home when a position opened up to head a major group. Traditionally, this position was a stepping-stone to senior partner status. Yet even though Don lobbied for the job, it went to Samir, who was two years Don's junior and had been at the firm for only eight years. Don had eyed and angled for this slot, and it was gone so quickly. The more he thought about it, the more he blamed not only Samir but also blamed his bosses, who had given him signals a few years back that he would get the promotion. Early on, he had heard many times that he was the perfect fit for the job. Perhaps they were telling him what they thought he wanted to hear.

Don reached down into the lower drawer of his office desk, where he kept his résumé. But it wasn't his own résumé that he was looking for, it was Samir's—he had managed to get his hands on it when he learned that he and Samir were both candidates for the position. He studied Samir's work record and compared it with his own, trying to discern why Samir was considered better qualified than he was. As he did so, he realized how he might look to an outside observer—like someone who was so desperately competitive that he had actually purloined his colleague's résumé. And like someone who was so angry and resentful that he continued to stare at Samir's résumé as if it might hold the answer to why his own career had stalled.

Don was apoplectic when he returned home that night. He vowed to his wife that he would quit rather than subject himself to further humiliation. "They just take me for granted," Don told her. "I deserved that job. I paid my dues."

The next day, Don confronted his boss about the situation. His boss didn't want to deal with Don's anger but he also didn't want to lose him, so he brought in an outside coach to work with him. Don reluctantly agreed to talk to the coach but still was hurt and resentful, and began exploring other job options. The coach, however, was good and had talked to a number of Don's colleagues prior to their first meeting. He had discovered that Don had turned down a number of opportunities offered to him by the firm. On two occasions, he'd declined to attend global leadership development programs—the firm was doing an increasing amount of overseas work and wanted to increase its global expertise. Don had also been reluctant to work with the firm's growing number of high-tech clients, claiming that he wasn't on the same wavelength as those "Silicon Valley guys" and suggesting that younger, more tech-savvy members of the firm should have these assignments. Finally, Don had demonstrated little interest in developing his own people. Despite the firm's emphasis on nurturing inside talent, Don rarely took the time to teach and facilitate his associates' self-awareness of their strengths and weaknesses—he expected them to learn these things on their own.

When the coach talked to Don about these issues, Don was initially defensive. He rationalized his unwillingness to take on these responsibilities, insisting that he should be doing what he did best and not wasting the firm's money in areas outside of his expertise.

It took a long time and a lot of work with the coach before he finally recognized what the real problem was: Don didn't want to do anything that might make him look bad. As he said, "I was a straight A student all my life. I was always on the fast track at this firm, and my work was always superior. I was afraid that if I tried something new I would look dumb in front of those Silicon Valley clients. And I was nervous about having those open and honest conversations with my own people—I've never been good at touchy-feely stuff."

In short, Don was a *high-need-for-achievement professional* who also had a high need to protect himself. He wanted to stick with his strengths and never expose his weaknesses. As a result, he had created his own career wall and subsequently hit it hard, as fast-trackers tend to do.

Are you, like Don, a high-need-for-achievement individual who has found yourself in a similar position? Or, if you haven't suffered his fate yet, do you see it as a possibility in the future?

Let me assure you that if you are like Don, this condition isn't fatal to your career. Even better, no matter how driven you are, you can avoid the traps that your drive creates and achieve career satisfaction. To avoid these traps and achieve this success, however, you need to be aware of two key issues:

- How your high-need-for-achievement personality can cause you to sabotage your career without even knowing it.

- How a dynamic process exists that can help you understand why you sabotage yourself and how you can rise above it to find the achievement and fulfillment you seek.

The chapter is divided into two sections that correspond to these issues. Let's begin by introducing the eleven traits of high-need-for-achievement types so you can see if any (or all) resonate with you.

Why Your Drive Can Cause You to Stall

Mark, a well-known CEO, told me of the time he visited his brother in a drug treatment center. This was the third time Mark's brother, a highly successful physician, had attempted to break his addiction to prescription drugs. Mark said that he would always remember the experience of being confronted by his brother during a family group session. As they sat in the circle his brother said to him, "Mark, there really isn't much difference between us. We are both addicts but of a different kind. My addiction ruined my first family and my career, and

I'm still trying to salvage it after thirty years of struggle. And your addiction to achieve and succeed has made you famous. But just realize that the difference between us is minimal."

When teaching various groups of executives, I relate the story of Mark and his brother. Each group responds similarly. They relate to these two professionally successful men and see that they live largely on the edge of their own insatiable need to keep achieving at all costs. They realize that they often shoot themselves in the foot because of their need to cross achievement markers off their lists—activities, assignments, and projects. And they also realize that their lists of things to do keep getting longer and longer the more they achieve. One newly minted doctor named Sara who was in the process of setting up her practice said, "I should have realized sooner that the more I cross off accomplishments and activities on the top of the page the more I add things to the bottom. My worry is whether or not this is going to be the pattern for my life. If I keep this up, all I will be at the end of my life is tired." Paul, a professor friend, once took me into his office and pointed out a pile of notepads that had accumulated over his thirty-year career. He had kept all his "to-do" lists, and each list was filled with crossed-out items signifying that they had been accomplished. Paul said, "Maybe at my funeral I should have these notepads stacked next to my casket as a way of showing what my life was all about."

This need to achieve is one of the central psychosocial needs that psychologists have been studying for years. Such needs or social motives are very different from physiological needs as defined by Abraham Maslow. Maslow suggests that our physiological needs can be extinguished temporarily through obvious and simple interventions. If we are thirsty we can drink water, and the need is extinguished for the time being. The same holds true for sleep, eating, sex, and so forth. Psychological theorist David McClelland, however, describes our psychosocial needs as producing the exact opposite effect. In other words, as we strive to meet our needs to achieve, the need becomes greater and greater.[1] It fact, it becomes insatiable, so that the more we achieve, the more we want to achieve. It also makes it difficult to do anything else other than think about or do work.

Some professionals live with the false assumption that once they achieve a certain amount of status, financial security, titles, or homes they will be satisfied to throttle back the drive to achieve. But the research says otherwise. This need to accomplish will persist forever. One of my clients, Sam, told me that he had the goal of achieving a certain net worth (a very big number) before he was sixty. Once he achieved it at age fifty-seven, however, he simply recalibrated his number upward and continued driving for the adjusted number. Kavita Wentworth, a leading Wall Street analyst, reported a similar experience when she built her second home in a resort town. Once it was completed she became frustrated with her older "full-time" home and began redecorating it from top to bottom. The last time we spoke she was considering buying another house so she would have places both in a warm-weather and cold-weather port.

I don't write this to insult you—as you no doubt realize, I'm a driven professional myself—but to state a truth that has escaped a lot of high-need-for-achievement people I know. In fact, the positive aspects of this personality type make your success possible. If you didn't have an insatiable desire for achievement and weren't so task focused, you would not have done as well as you have. But ambition can be blinding, and when you're so obsessed with completing tasks effectively and maintaining your stature within the organization, you may miss some critical aspects that define you—and that can keep you from achieving the success you seek.

Therefore, let's examine eleven traits common to driven professionals that often cause them problems in terms of career success and satisfaction:

- Being driven to achieve the task

- Failing to differentiate "urgent" from merely "important"

- Having difficulty with delegating

- Struggling with producer-to-supervisor transition

- Obsessing about getting the job done at all costs

- Avoiding difficult conversations

- Craving feedback

- Swinging from one mood extreme to another

- Comparing

- Taking only safe risks

- Feeling guilty

Being Driven to Achieve the Task

Individuals with a high need for achievement are motivated by superior performance. They want to do a job as well as it's ever been
done, if not better. The most fundamental motivator is the need for
task challenge. They hunger for jobs that push them, where they have
tough problems that they must solve. They relish helping their bosses
or clients through task accomplishment. In general, if the work is te-
dious or repetitive, they become unmotivated, start blaming others
for their predicament, or get depressed because they feel like they
are falling behind others. Even worse, they become absolutely convinced that their friends and colleagues are doing a much better job
than they are of leveraging their talents and growing by leaps and
bounds while they are stagnating. In short, they become caught up in
their tasks and fight against anything—transparency, empathy, etc.—

that doesn't help them directly with the superior accomplishment of the task.

Failing to Differentiate
"Urgent" from Merely "Important"

Problems with differentiating between what is important and what is urgent is another characteristic these driven professionals share. Nancy, an accountant, said that she became nervous whenever she reviewed all the tasks she listed on her to-do list; all of them seemed equally urgent and important. The notion of downgrading any of the items to a less urgent category struck her as unbearable. When Nancy arrived at work in the morning, everything on her list seemed equally important: watering the plants, giving a performance evaluation to a subordinate, and creating a final presentation for an important meeting in the afternoon. Even when she managed to cross an item off her list, she felt compelled to add other items to replace them. In a frenzied state where even relatively minor responsibilities loomed large, Nancy couldn't take a step back to reflect. Perhaps even more important, she was unable to have an honest and in-depth conversation with her colleagues; she lacked the time and focus to think about and respond to what was important to someone else.

Having Difficulty with Delegating

High achievers get such a thrill from accomplishing the task at hand that they find it difficult to delegate. Taking the time to teach others slows down their own process of achievement. They are also one step removed from the specific task at hand if someone else accomplishes it instead. And at a deeper, more psychological level, people who relish crossing items off the list worry that if they delegate tasks, their subordinates won't be able to accomplish the task as well as they would have. One professional admitted, "I hate to state out loud that I think

I can do something better than anyone else, but I really think at some fundamental level I believe it. I know it can't be true, but the way I hold on to tasks make me wonder whether I really trust anyone else to do it better than I." Obviously, delegating requires a certain degree of vulnerability, since you have to extend trust that others will meet your high standards. The other challenge of delegating centers on the time it will take to sit down and teach someone else how to do a particular project. If the boss slows down his productivity in order to teach, he can become frustrated because he's accomplishing less, at least in the short term.

Struggling with Producer-to-Supervisor Transition

High achievers also worry that if they give up their technical functional work or expertise for a more supervisory position, they may lose their ability to do the work. Dalton and Thompson's research identified the challenge that individual contributors had in moving to the next stage of a career. Moving from stage 2 (technical functional competence) to mentor becomes a huge psychological hurdle; people's self-concept is wrapped up in being great at doing something thoroughly and well.[2] The thought of giving up this technical superiority in exchange for managing others is scary. The assumption is that these individuals, who are technically competent, will be good at managing because they have illustrated that they are good at producing. This assumption, however, doesn't reflect many new managers' realities; they often find that learning to manage is like learning to speak a different language. As a result, some of them micromanage while others continue to be individual contributors despite their managerial titles; both behaviors irritate their direct reports and prevent them from learning and growing in a new role.

The other reality is that managing and mentoring others is harder to measure than performing a specific task. How do you know if your feedback to a direct report is doing any good? How do you measure the "softer" skills of being a manager that have longer-term implications and fewer short-term outcomes? High-need-for-achievement personalities struggle with these managerial facts of life, and their struggle prevents them from focusing on long-term goals, which drives them a bit batty.

Obsessing About Getting the Job Done at All Costs

Driven professionals possess tunnel vision when it comes to getting jobs done with all due speed and effectiveness. They're very impatient with any obstacle or anyone who gets in the way of reaching the desired outcome. One doctor admitted that he became frustrated with those who got in the way of his crossing things off his list—who prevented him from finishing a task when he wanted to do it or assembling the resources necessary to purchase state-of-the-art medical technology. This was also true when he was home and his young children didn't achieve what he felt they should achieve, such as getting certain grades at school—it got in the way of his crossing things off his list as a parent. Getting things done is difficult when there are interruptions, like the need to coach or mentor a younger doctor, for example, or taking a few minutes to give feedback to another person. When you're task driven like this doctor, you want to finish the examination and procedure quickly and expertly. Getting these tasks done well and efficiently is what is motivating and energizing short term.

Avoiding Difficult Conversations

I know about avoiding difficult conversations from hard experience. Years ago, Steve, a younger associate, and I had made a presentation to a client, and we didn't get the business. Though this was disappointing, it wasn't as disappointing as my lack of courage and urgency in giving feedback to Steve immediately. We had flown to Chicago for the presentation, and I thought Steve was clear about what he would present. During the meeting, though, he departed from our prearranged agenda and addressed a topic we had not planned to include in the presentation. I could tell that he was going down a path that might be counterproductive, and I should have stopped him. But I didn't.

Even worse, on the trip back home, I failed to explain to Steve the mistake he had made. As I look back now, I can rationalize why I didn't speak up. I had phone calls to make. I needed to text a dozen people before we got to the plane. I was worried about the weather. I needed to return to Boston for a family activity. The list went on. But by delaying a simple but honest conversation I set the stage for a future encounter that proved more unsettling than the botched meeting and subsequent failure to be honest with Steve and truly manage him.

Nearly eight months later, in December, it was time for performance reviews. When Steve came to my office, I asked him if he remembered the trip to Chicago, and he said, "Of course." I then began to tell him what he had done wrong during the presentation: "Steve, when we met with the private equity firm in Chicago last April you skipped the most important part of the presentation and went on to something that really wasn't helpful." Steve just stared at me. Before he replied I could see that his face was turning red. He responded in a hurt tone, explaining why he had made the presentation the way he had. After what seemed like an hour (and was probably no more than ten seconds), I offered a defensive response to his response—I told him how busy I was that day and that the conversation just got pushed to the side.

Though I said this in a matter-of-fact manner, I felt embarrassed and exposed. I felt that I had been caught in a lie or at least a deception. My voice might have been steady, but the rest of me was not. My face felt hot. My hands began to sweat. Steve, who had always trusted me, was literally pulling away from me, edging his chair back. I thought I knew exactly what he was thinking. The words that should have been coming out of his mouth were, "Why didn't you tell me then? I thought we had a close relationship. I trusted you explicitly and this is what I get." In just a few minutes, I had changed the nature of a relationship from one that was based on high engagement and great commitment to one that was perfunctory and contractual in nature. Or at least that is how Steve began to think and act. What made it worse is that I tried to cover myself. Instead of leveling with him and having an honest and open conversation, I was defensive. I was again afraid of being vulnerable.

In the past when a boss had let me down, I had made assumptions about the boss's behavior. I could imagine Steve reflecting: "Now I know why Tom took another colleague with him on those two other trips to meet clients. Now I know why he spent less time with me in the last few months. Now I know why Tom had dinner with two other colleagues and I wasn't invited." These were all fiction, but in Steve's mind they all seemed like facts. They were logical conclusions based on how I acted during and after our presentation in Chicago and the performance review eight months later.

I never was able to establish a trusting relationship with Steve again. This hurt Steve, it hurt the company, and it hurt me. Steve left the firm a few months later. And I believe to this day that it happened because I was myopically focused on accomplishing short-term tasks at the expense of longer-term relationships. I wanted to get my short-term tasks done come hell or high water. And—yes—I feared having an honest conversation. As a result, I wasn't open and honest with Steve. I didn't want to deal with the messy, nontask issues involved in an awkward, uncomfortable conversation. I didn't want to be vulnerable and admit that I had made a mistake.

Craving Feedback

High-need-for-achievement personalities crave feedback more than the general population as a whole. They want to perform as well as possible, which in turn means getting feedback on what they are not doing well and what they could do to improve. Though these individuals want feedback, they don't always respond well to it, especially when it's negative. That's partly because they so rarely hear bad things about their performance. Negative feedback hurts them deeply because they feel like they are not meeting expectations or perceived expectations. They are hardwired to try and exceed expectations at all costs. They want to please everyone all the time and when that doesn't happen, they manipulate their environment so they hear what they want to hear at the time they want to hear it from the person they want to hear it from. In other words, though they want feedback, they are unwilling to make themselves sufficiently vulnerable to take it in objectively and deeply; they fail to display the resilience to learn from the feedback and improve how they handle similar situations the next time. One reflective leader told me, "When I'm discouraged I know exactly who to go to who will tell me how great I am so that I quit feeling sorry for myself. I've never sat down consciously and figured out how I construct my environment to reinforce all my tendencies, but I'm sure it wouldn't take me long to do it."

Swinging from One Extreme Mood to Another

Why don't high achievers want critical feedback? If they're smart and have achieved a certain amount of success, why can't they just deal with the truth? Two reasons: self-loathing and self-criticism. This is one end of their mood spectrum, and they often swing to this end with surprising speed, as we will see.

Figure 1-1 illustrates how a normal distribution of the population deals with accomplishing tasks, being responsible, and taking in feedback. At one tail of the distribution are individuals who are hyper-self-critical when it comes to following through and accomplishing tasks. At the other end of the distribution is a subgroup defined as hyperresponsible.

FIGURE 1-1

The anxiety curve

When high-need-for-achievement personalities trip and perceive that they have been less than successful, they move quickly from seeing themselves as responsible to seeing themselves as failures. They move from an 8 or 10 to 1 or 2 in their own minds.

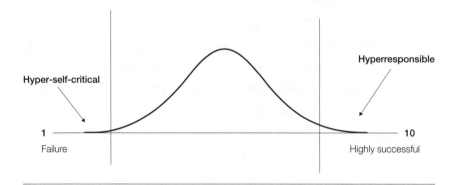

John J. Gabarro, a former colleague, describes hyperresponsible individuals as having a need to please anyone and everyone. They want to accomplish everything that is assigned to them. They want to exceed expectations on every project. The better they meet and exceed expectations, the more they are asked to do and—to a large extent—the more they thrive. However, when these individuals begin to stumble even a little bit, rather than shrugging off the stumble they begin to believe they are failures. If they see themselves as highly competent and confident, when they perceive that they have violated the expectations of someone or let someone down, they see themselves as failures. They can question their overall performance, their career choice, their network, their support system.[3] One friend said, "When I'm down on myself and question my abilities, I find myself criticizing every part of my life. Thank goodness my children are handsome because I could even imagine myself beginning to see my kids as ugly. It gets that pathetic when I'm hypercritical of myself. Everything is bleak."

Such driven individuals then respond by trying to do anything to receive positive feedback or to be told that they are really competent. They receive positive reinforcement by manipulating their environment; they jump up the positive self-regard scale to a point where they can continue accomplishing tasks. In short order, they rebound from negative feedback or a setback with alacrity, and to observers they appear remarkably resilient and confident.

This particular mood-swing trait is readily identifiable, especially by people who live with these highly ambitious individuals. Driven professionals can be very difficult to live with because the significant people in their lives never know what kind of mood they will be in when they return from work. But they come to know they will get an extreme. Someone will walk in the door feeling on top of the world and able to handle anything in life or someone will burst in being hyper-critical, tense, easily irritated, highly opinionated, and communicating "Beware." One close friend admitted that his moods were so obvious that his children knew by the way he closed the car door whether he was approachable. When interviewed, his kids said, "If dad closed the door softly then we headed for our rooms because he would be looking for trouble. If he closed the door firmly we knew we could run to embrace him and tease him and begin asking for attention or things or simply time."

Comparing

This trait is a central theme of the book, and later I will discuss in detail the process of comparison or social relativity. For our purposes here, however, recognize that calibrating accomplishments in the context of how others do is a trap; it prevents people from changing behavior and becoming vulnerable. People compare their performance with others according to career stage, age, and generation. Their ability to calibrate themselves accurately is closely related to the quality of the feedback they receive and how much they manipulate their environments to hear what they want to hear. Many high achievers will seek other opportunities if they can't calibrate their comparative performance/achievement factors rather easily. They may request a job transfer, leave an organization, or even seek work in another industry if they struggle to know how they're doing relative to others. They also may arrive at a false calibration because they frequently allow their biases or blind spots to color their comparisons, whether consciously or not.

Taking Only Safe Risks

Taking only safe risks is paradoxical, since high achievers relish seizing opportunistic risks to get ahead, yet they are also risk averse to the extent that they are fearful of taking a risk and failing. High-achiever types manage this paradox by being both perceptive about risk and selective about risks they take. More specifically, they are calculated risk takers. They can figure out the odds of a risk paying off, and if the odds seem favorable, they'll take a gamble (though it's not really much of a gamble, since they've made sure the odds are in their favor). Ask any lawyer in a top-tier law firm whether attorneys are risk takers. The same holds true for accountants. Or financial services professionals. Or consultants. Their source of motivation is related to their need for task challenge, but they are motivated only by challenges that are realistic and achievable.

One lawyer in a top London-based law firm said, "Tom, you need to realize that the last thing a smart lawyer wants to be seen as is incompetent or stupid. Embarrassment is devastating. We lawyers will do anything to make sure that we save face, that we manage our environment so that we don't look foolish." When challenges and assignments don't seem achievable, driven professionals balk. Balking translates into wondering if they can accomplish the task, becoming anxious and tense about the outcome, and handling a stretch assignment without sufficient confidence. High-need-for-achievement professionals are loath to experience the negative feelings that come with blowing an important but risky project. When this happens, their self-talk verges on the abusive; they beat themselves up mercilessly. While they might provide negative feedback to a subordinate who takes a bad risk, their feedback to themselves is much worse. Therefore, high achievers make sure that they can achieve the tasks that they set out to do. As long as they only take calculated risks, they can avoid feeling vulnerable.

Feeling Guilty

Achievement-driven personalities are inherently ambitious, and as a result, they take on many assignments. The more tasks they put on their list, the more likely they'll experience what Jack Gabarro describes as role overload and inter-role conflict. *Role overload* means recognizing that you have more roles and responsibilities than are achievable, and you start choosing one role over another. *Inter-role* conflict means that when one role is chosen over another, other responsibilities are ignored. When this happens, these driven professionals begin to experience ongoing guilt because all their tasks cannot be accomplished. So these individuals live lives where each day begins with the chronic feeling that they should be doing something else and that no matter what they do they won't have enough time.[4]

It is difficult for these people to enjoy their work and their careers when they feel guilty all the time. It is also difficult to be transparent and admit feeling guilty since there's the fear that people will see them as lazy or unable to handle the job. Thus, despite this roiling sense of inadequacy on the inside, these individuals present a brave, false front to the outside world.

Assessing the Eleven Traits

As you read through the descriptions of each of the eleven traits, you may have thought to yourself, "I do that."

Just because these traits are common, however, doesn't mean that they have to derail your career. In fact, just becoming aware of them will go a long way toward preventing them from doing damage. Once you become more conscious of these tendencies, you'll be able to change your behaviors to more productive ones. To that end, I've compiled a group of questions that you should ask yourself to assess which traits are impeding your career progress and job satisfaction:

- Being driven to achieve the task
  - Do you find yourself dissatisfied with your performance if you only do a satisfactory job? Even when you do a good job, do you often beat yourself up because you believe you could have done better?
  - Do you regularly cast an envious eye on the careers of your friends? Do you believe that they're doing better than you, no matter how well you're doing?
  - Are you constantly looking for roles and responsibilities that challenge you? Do you feel you need to prove yourself by tackling assignments with high degrees of difficulty?

- Failing to differentiate urgency from merely important
  - Do you find it difficult to prioritize your to-do list? Does it seem impossible to designate whether one item on it is less important than others?
  - Is it likely that you find yourself trying to do everything at once? Do you spread yourself thin attempting to get multiple tasks done simultaneously because you can't figure out which task demands your full attention?

- Having difficulty with delegating
  - How often do you take over a task that you initially assigned to someone else? Do you do so because you don't believe

the direct report can handle the task or because you become anxious that he can't do it as well as you can?

- When you do manage to delegate an assignment, do you constantly check up on that person and micromanage her work?

- Are you reluctant to delegate because you don't like wasting the time necessary to teach someone else to do something?

- Struggling with producer-to-supervisor transition

  - Do you find your managerial role uncomfortable and confusing, especially contrasted with your individual contributor role?

  - When you try to manage others, do you struggle to know how well you're doing? Does the lack of clear measures bother you?

  - Are you surprised that while you thought you would be a good manager, you either don't like to manage or you realize you may not be as good at it as you thought you would be?

- Obsessing about getting the job done at all costs

  - Do you lie awake nights wondering about how you're going to be able to meet deadlines?

  - Are you always trying to figure out ways to get things done faster (even when your current pace is fine)?

  - Are you willing to push both yourself and your people to the limit to accomplish a task?

- Avoiding difficult conversations

  - When you know you have to tell someone something that will make one or both of you uncomfortable, do you postpone it for as long as you can? Do you sometimes manage to avoid this conversation entirely?

- Do you sugar-coat performance reviews to avoid arguments and defensive reactions?

- Are you often willing to accept a less-than-favorable outcome rather than engage in a dialogue that might produce a better outcome?

- Craving feedback

  - Are you constantly looking for people to tell you how you did? Do you manipulate your environment so you receive just the feedback you want?

  - Are you fearful of negative feedback? Do you try to avoid conversations with those who might say something about your performance that will upset you?

  - Do you have a group of people or one particular individual who you seek out for feedback because you know you will be given a positive response?

- Swinging from one mood extreme to another

  - Do you tend to be either very high or very low, and spend very little time in the emotional range in between?

  - Are you likely to overreact to mild criticism from a boss and think you'll be fired the next day? Are you likely to exaggerate mild praise from a boss and believe you'll receive the next big promotion?

- Comparing

  - Do you find yourself thinking about your achievements and career only in relative terms? Do they only mean something to you in relation to how others in your position have done?

- When you find it difficult to measure your performance, do you reflexively look for another job or another position in the company where measures are more apparent?

- Taking only safe risks

  - Do you feel that you stack the deck in your favor when you take on what others perceive to be a challenging assignment? Are you reasonably sure that you can complete an assignment effectively before you take it on?

  - Do you do everything possible to avoid risks if you might end up with egg on your face? Do you stay away from certain assignments because you know that they're tough and you may not look good while working on them?

- Feeling guilty

  - Even if you're working hard and getting a lot accomplished, do you feel as if you aren't doing enough and that you could handle more responsibility, despite appearances to the contrary?

  - Does every break from the action cause you to feel lazy or slow? Do you feel you don't want to take a vacation because you will get behind? Does a long lunch make you feel like you're slacking off?

  - When you work an eight- instead of a twelve-hour day, do you remonstrate with yourself because you've "taken it easy"? Do you believe that you're letting down the company, your team, and yourself?

CHAPTER TWO

The Challenge of Doing the Right Thing Poorly

A S YOU ANSWERED THE QUESTIONS that closed chapter 1, you might have found yourself wondering about the significance of your answers. In other words, what can you do with the knowledge that you struggle with delegating and that you crave feedback? Aren't you always going to operate with a high-need-for-achievement motor?

Of course, but you don't always have to allow this need to back you into a corner or wear you down. Many ambitious professionals over-come the obstacles they place in their paths by fitting their behaviors into a manageable context. By that I mean that they learn to see the pattern of their behaviors and how to adjust that pattern so it's pro-ductive rather than counterproductive.

The traits you exhibit as a driven professional form a dynamic—a predictable pattern of behaviors that can lead you in positive or nega-tive directions. This dynamic will be illustrated through three charts in this section, but before showing them to you I want to describe this dynamic in words.

The Anxiety Pit

Let's start out by reflecting on your responses to the previous questions. If you're like most high-need-for-achievement professionals, just thinking about your answers made you anxious. They prompted you to consider what you might do differently. They raised the possibility that you might have to change in order to be more successful and more satisfied in your work. That's scary, because change means we cannot look or feel as if we're in total control. Better to wallow in anxiety rather than subject ourselves to honest self-examination; at least this way we can maintain control. Though we may present a strong image to the outside world, inside, questions are roiling about our purpose, our significance, our feelings of loneliness.

As high-need-for-achievement individuals, we become enmeshed in our anxieties. In other words, we get in our own way. Change provides a path through the mire, and even those in positions of power and influence need to find this path.

Unfortunately, everyone—from top business executives to big law firm partners to investment gurus to individual business owners to full-time day-care providers—tends to become stuck in personal anxieties rather than move through them. Ministering to these anxieties may provide some short-term comfort, but eventually such subservience catches up with us. When we're deeply and consistently anxious, we can't face the truth; we hear just what we want to hear. One former leader opined, "I waited too long to hear what I needed to hear. I figured out a way fairly early in life to seek situations and people who would reinforce the messages I wanted to hear. I was forty years old before I realized that I could break this pathetic cycle and learn what I needed to learn. I became so fearful of what I might be told that I basically froze up internally."

An HR leader from the field of organizational behavior provided me with an insightful explanation about how anxiety stymies many bright professionals. He suggested a dichotomy between the worries professionals talk about and focus on—their salaries, their perks, their companies overall—and the worries that are more personal in nature. These latter can include relationships with a boss and colleagues, concerns about their own learning and development, and their sense of meaning and fulfillment. When leaders don't address these concerns—when they focus on satisfying the close-to-the-surface worries about salary and titles—their people become fixated on their personal anxieties. They are so anxious that they stop taking risks and having open and honest conversations and instead think only about how they can avoid the next downsizing or how to stay in their boss's good graces. They stop learning and growing . . . and achieving.

One executive found that the professionals he observed over thirty years were highly anxious because they wanted but weren't receiving honest feedback. There were other reasons as well—they weren't being recognized, they didn't feel included, they believed that they were not making enough progress. The executive asked his employees, "On your darkest days, why do you think about leaving? And on your darkest days, why do you stay?" Their answers revealed that though they were *attracted* to the company because of the compensation they received, the particular industry, and the company's standing in the marketplace, they remained *committed* because they felt significant, purposeful, and included—and they considered leaving when these feelings were absent.

The point is that now, more than ever before, organizations fail to make even their high-need-for-achievement people feel included and valued. If you work for a large company, it's likely you feel more anxious today than you ever did in the past. And if you work for yourself or for a small company, the current volatile and uncertain environment contributes to your anxiety; you feel excluded by new technology you don't understand or by the push to be global when you're happy being local.

In fact, if you're like most driven professionals I know, you have so much anxiety that you would give even Woody Allen pause. Despite your outward appearance of calm and control, inside you're neurotically fearful. And so, you rarely take behavioral risks, seldom open up to others, and often fail to empathize or listen deeply to others. You may survive, but at what cost? You seldom feel good about what you do. You don't learn and grow and enjoy becoming more than you were before. You never reach your performance potential.

FIGURE 2-1

The growth pyramid

Only by moving from the upper-left corner of the inverted pyramid to the bottom tip can you reach the ultimate goal of being vulnerable and open to possibilities.

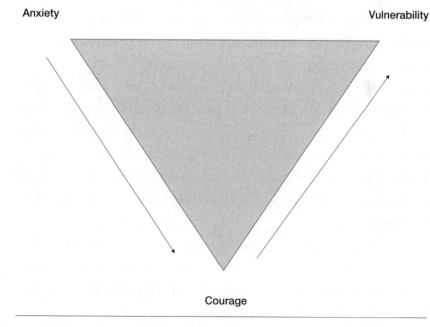

Anxiety   Vulnerability

Courage

Figure 2-1 represents the fear that keeps you from change, the courage that's required to overcome the fear and the vulnerability that's necessary for change to happen.

Each point of the triangle represents a point in the journey, and many bright, ambitious professionals become stuck at point 1 (anxiety). As we have experiences throughout life, we build up anxieties that paralyze us. Instead of digging ourselves out of these psychological holes, we fall into traps that take us to the deeper parts of these holes. At some point, though, we decide to stop digging and start climbing. We build up enough courage to see a glimmer of possibilities. We reach out to someone who invests in us psychologically and spiritually and, with courage as our mantra, adopt an attitude of learning and vulnerability.

Doing the Right Thing

Here is a Tiger Woods story that has nothing to do with his relatively recent marital problems. Instead, it recalls a time when Woods was in his ascendancy, about to become arguably the greatest golfer the sport had ever known.

Tiger Woods won the 1997 Masters Tournament in Augusta, Georgia, by twelve strokes. It was such an overwhelming victory that Augusta National redesigned its course to increase the odds that Woods would not repeat the feat. Yet after Woods won the tournament, his coach, Butch Harmon, told him that, while he had played superb golf for four days he had a problem with his swing. He suggested that Woods needed to rebuild his swing from the ground up. Harman admitted that Woods could win sporadically without a change but would never challenge the greats like Jack Nicklaus.

Put yourself in Woods's position. Would you be willing to rebuild your swing after such significant success? Consider whether you have the courage to admit that despite your career success up to this point,

FIGURE 2-2

Breaking the cycle

By moving to the lower right quadrant from either quadrant on the left, you begin the process of change.

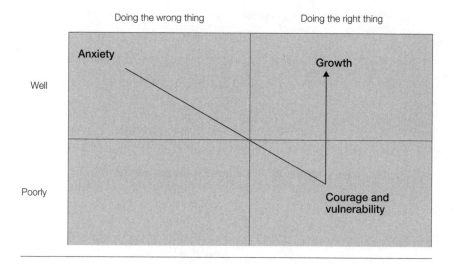

you need to develop a new competency and risk appearing less-than-stellar as you master it?

Figure 2-2, a 2 × 2 matrix, provides four options for performance. If you want to follow a path to growth, you can't avoid the stage where you're vulnerable. Examine the matrix, and you'll see that you have the opportunity to do the wrong thing well or the wrong thing poorly; you also have the choice to do the right thing well or poorly. Most people perceive the upper right quadrant as the place to be, since doing the right thing well seems like the quadrant that will lead to significant achievement. It is a great feeling to master some skill set and perform it the correct way at the right time and in the appropriate context. The challenge is how to get to the point where you can do the right thing well. How do you get to this quadrant?

The only way to get there is through the bottom right quadrant. The only way you can do something well is to do something poorly first. There is no other way. That means being vulnerable. But that also means learning and pursuing satisfaction and growth where change is possible.

During the final moments of a four-day program, I told the Tiger Woods story to a group of executives. Right after I finished the story, a forty-five-year-old executive raised his hand and confronted me in front of the group. He said, "Professor DeLong, I don't like your story about Tiger Woods. I don't think the story is fair." I wanted to cut him down with a cynical reply. My palms started sweating. I experienced shortness of breath. I managed to ask him why it wasn't a fair story. He responded, "Professor, the reason your story isn't fair is that Tiger Woods was able to work on his swing and go to the lower right quadrant and only his coach was there. There was only one person there to watch him do poorly. I have forty-five hundred employees in my company, and if I try anything new they will all see me. It could be humiliating. I have to set an example of doing the right thing well all the time." I didn't really know what to say. The room became very quiet. Students waited for me to react. I realized that the silence was the best teacher. I simply said, "I guess you are right."

The executive had made a great observation about Tiger Woods and himself. The fundamental question out there for all to see, was whether this leader or any of the participants in the group realized what it would take to get over themselves and be courageous enough to try something that they might not be initially competent in. The challenge this executive had raised for the whole class was now in the open. I realized that for high-need-for-achievement personalities, looking good and managing image are primary concerns; the last thing these people want is to look dumb or anything other than very competent.

Years ago I resented Nike's advertising campaign "Image Is Everything." I wondered how any company could make such a blatant fallacy a major marketing theme. Then I grasped that Nike's marketing team was just being honest. They were making me very uncomfortable because I knew at some level that the truth hurts. In the fast-paced world we live in, image *is* everything. Whether we're young managers or senior executives, we don't want to tarnish that image. Unfortunately, this means that we're sentencing ourselves to a superficial existence, that we can't change our behaviors and try something that makes us uncomfortable because we're worried how we'll look to the people that surround us. So rather than doing the right thing poorly until we get better, we resign ourselves to doing the wrong thing well over and over again.

I'm not suggesting that it's easy to do the right thing poorly on our way to doing it well. One leader told me that when he got home he treated his family like subordinates. He knew his dictatorial behavior wasn't good at work and it wasn't good at home, but he continued to act inappropriately because he couldn't or wouldn't make the leap. And it is a leap. Imagine what must have gone through this leader/dictator's mind as he considered changing his behaviors: "What if I try to be more fair-minded and encourage participatory decision making? My people will take advantage of me and whisper that I'm getting weak. My kids will rebel and get in all sorts of trouble and think I'm a pushover."

Even when we do start to change, we are tempted to regress to old ways. It is like having bungee cords tied around our waist, dragging us back to the old, ineffective, habit-induced behavior. When we begin to feel nervous and self-conscious—when our anxieties ratchet up a notch or two—we know we are getting close to experiencing something real. And that's when we often step back rather than move forward. Technically competent professionals like accountants, programmers, lawyers, engineers, surgeons, investment bankers, and great athletes are especially vulnerable to embarrassment. Looking stupid is the enemy. Why else do these smart people become more and more anxious the further they get away from their comfort zone?

Actually, preserving their image is only one motivation. Another involves negative institutional sanctions. Organizations do not always reward trying something different even if leadership endorses innovation and prudent risk taking. Leaders speak out of both sides of their mouths. They want it both ways. One leader I know confided, "My boss wants innovation and risk taking as long as it's done perfectly the first time." Or as another senior executive complained, "We say over and over again that we will support innovation, but if it doesn't work out the first time we alienate or isolate the innovators and finger point. We basically push them over the cliff or shun them or talk about them behind their backs or mock them."

People also resist getting over themselves and trying something new because of a perceived cost beyond a tarnished image. Instead, it could be a cost in relationships, competence, or skill level. Some organizations don't want to invest in moving professionals from one silo to another. These people could be high producers, and rather than give them the opportunity to have a global experience or an adventure in another division, they are told to stay put in the interest of short-term profits. Forget the long-term benefits for the organization and the individual who is developing new, essential skills. If that person insists on taking on a new assignment, he may lose his relationships with his superiors, his stature within the organization, and even his new job.

Even when smart professionals try something new, they often are their own worst enemies, retreating to the safety of doing the wrong thing well. As fast-trackers accustomed to picking up skills quickly and receiving immediate rewards, they have difficulty dealing with slow learning curves. One friend told me he quit playing golf because he couldn't master the sport playing only three times a year. He reported that he was playing at the famous Winged Foot Golf Club in Westchester County, N.Y., when he picked up his ball on the fourth hole and told his playing partners that he was through. He was so disgusted with himself and his game that he left the course and left a note for his friends that he would see them at work on Monday.

Moving to the lower right quadrant is also challenging because we don't always know the perfect path to the upper right quadrant. We are not always sure what lies ahead, particularly in organizations. Take, for example, lawyers who joined a prestigious law firm twenty years ago. The clients may have lined up outside their office door. There may have not been a need to sell work. Instead, it came to them. But then the legal world changed. Overnight, the competition for work picked up. Lawyers are now expected to not only *do* the work but *sell* the work. Some of these older lawyers now feel left out in the cold. The rules have changed and the bar has moved. The same phenomenon has happened in the world of investment banking. Investment bankers have to hustle work, and that doesn't always sit well. Their worlds changed, as did their definition of the upper right quadrant; and if they had trouble defining that quadrant, how could they chart a path to the lower right quadrant?

Question Your Willingness to Do the Right Thing Poorly

It doesn't matter if you are just starting out in a career or if you're the most prominent leader in your industry. Most professionals from young consultants to CEOs are reluctant to try something new for fear they'll look dumb, awkward, hesitant, and so on. As a result, they stick with what they know at the expense of taking risks, stretching themselves, and being innovative. High-need-for-achievement professionals, no matter their titles or their experiences, often fail to question their willingness to do the right thing poorly.

Answer the following questions to determine your willingness to do the right thing poorly first, before heading to the upper right quadrant:

- How many significant behavioral or work changes have you made in the past ten years? How many times have you been brave enough to do something where you suspected you'd look stupid or at least unsure about what you were doing?

- If you were asked to compose a list of risks that you have taken in your work and your life, how many would there be on the list? How many have taken place in the last five years; in the last year?

- When you contemplate making a significant change in your job or career, what anxieties or concerns arise to stop you from following through? What are the consequences you fear most if you do make a change?

- Can you think of instances in the past few months when you've been completely honest and transparent with your colleagues, even if this stance didn't place you in the most flattering light? Can you recall even one instance during this period where you told your boss a hard truth, were completely honest with a direct report, or admitted your lack of knowledge or a mistake to a group of people?

Most people answer these questions in a way that demonstrates that their anxieties are preventing them from changing their routine behaviors. Recognizing this fact isn't cause for alarm. Instead, it's the first step on the road to awareness and change. As you can see when the triangle from figure 2-1 is overlaid on the matrix from figure 2-2, the journey from doing the wrong thing well to doing the right thing poorly is one from anxiety to courage (see figure 2-3). Without being brave enough to push back your anxiety and take a risk, you won't get to this lower right quadrant. Once there, you must embrace vulnerability as you learn new skills and acquire new knowledge and sometimes have to say, "I don't know." The reward for doing so, however, is taking the final leg of the journey to the upper right quadrant where you do the right thing well.

FIGURE 2-3

Growth pyramid in context

The two central models of the book—figures 2-1 and 2-2—integrate.

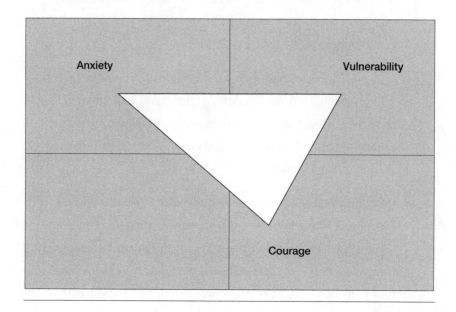

From Coach to Hero

I want to inspire you to let yourself be vulnerable, so let me end the chapter on this inspirational note.

Maurice Cheeks became notable as a professional basketball player for the Philadelphia 76ers in the '80s and early '90s. He was a good point guard who was skilled at passing the ball to the right team-mate at the right time. He eventually went on to be a coach, first for the Seattle Supersonics, then the Portland Trailblazers, and finally to his beloved 76ers until the beginning of the 2008–2009 season. But in 2004, when he coached the Trailblazers, there was a particular event that took place before a home game against the Dallas Mavericks that will always be connected with Coach Cheeks.

At the Rose Garden in Portland, Oregon, the traditional singing of the National Anthem began, with a young woman who had won a local singing contest doing the honors. A few bars into the anthem, though, she froze. She forgot the words. She began to stutter and stopped singing. The crowd was nervously silent. Time slowed to a crawl. The silence became deafening. And what was obvious was that everyone was paralyzed; no one was coming to her aid. All of a sudden, out of nowhere (actually from the other end of the court, where he was with his players), Cheeks approached the young, terrified woman and began to sing the words to the anthem. Almost immediately, the young woman came back to life and sang haltingly. Gradually she began to catch her stride and sang with more feeling. Cheeks was right there singing with her. The crowd at the Rose Garden began to sing. Loudly. The camera panned over to the opposing players and they were all singing. Don Nelson, the opposing coach, was singing. The referees were singing. The fans sang louder and louder. Every person in the arena was helping this woman with the words. You saw some people wiping their eyes. And Cheeks just kept singing. At the end of the song, Cheeks hugged the young woman and walked quickly back to his players and staff.

Cheeks taught us what it means to move to the lower right quadrant when the pressure is on. Cheeks is not a singer by any stretch of the imagination. I'm not sure he hit one right note, musically speaking. In fact, I've never heard such a bad voice; but do you think it mattered? Do you think anyone cared about the quality of his voice? No doubt, Cheeks experienced some anxiety as he walked toward the young woman. Yet he had the courage to start singing and make himself vulnerable. He got over and past himself. Despite his many accomplishments in areas where he's highly skilled and successful, I doubt there are many other moments of which he is prouder. It gave even greater meaning to an already successful life.

You can do the same thing that Maurice Cheeks did, albeit in a different, less conspicuous context. You can overcome your anxieties and change your behaviors. You can display the courage necessary to do the right thing poorly, followed by doing the right thing well, and learn and grow from that experience. As the the 2 × 2 matrix demonstrates, the path to success isn't a straight line, but rather one that requires a brief detour in an unexpected direction, one that provides the direction for greater professional and life satisfaction.

PART II

THE BIG

THREE

ANXIETIES

CHAPTER THREE

Purpose

What's It All About?

A S MUCH AS YOU MIGHT BE INSPIRED by Maurice Cheeks's example and want to do the right thing poorly first, doing it in a real work situation is the challenge. As you vow to take on a stretch assignment or to plunge into some task in which you know you'll struggle initially, something happens between the thought and the action. That something is anxiety.

More than one author has referred to our current era as "the age of anxiety," and you don't need to be trained in psychology to understand how deep-rooted and pervasive this mood is. While everyone suffers from the stress and strain of living in volatile times, high-need-for-achievement personalities are under particular pressure—much of it self-induced. Jobs are less secure; people are being asked to do more work in less time; competition for promotions is more intense; the bar has been raised on performance; employees come and go with alarming speed; consciousness has been raised about doing meaningful work; and many professionals are questioning what they do for a living. And some professionals may not have work and are particularly stressed. Whatever anxieties driven professionals already have are ratcheted up several notches in the current environment.

Anxiety operates like an emotional vise, tightening around hard-charging professionals and limiting their range. They may understand on some level that if they were able to display empathy, be more transparent, and admit when they did something wrong, they would be better at their jobs and more satisfied doing the work. Anxiety, though, often prevents people from exhibiting vulnerabilities. As we'll see, it keeps people locked in place, both literally and figuratively.

Of all the anxieties that professionals experience, *purpose*-related worries and fears are high on the list. If you're not quite sure how purpose can produce paralyzing anxiety, you need to understand what purpose really means and how this concept impacts professionals.

Here's What Purpose Is All About

The theme song of the 1970s cult movie *Alfie* is titled, "What's It All About?" For those individuals who seek a reason for being, this song can serve as a theme song as well. The three central fears and anxieties that drive dysfunctional behavior of individuals are:

- The lack of purpose and direction

- The sense of isolation or abandonment, being disconnected

- The feeling of insignificance (e.g., "Do I matter?")

In other words, does anyone but me care whether I belong to this organization, institution, or family? Does anybody but me care whether or not I show up to work? This lack of affirmation in interpersonal relationships and from organizations is scary. At a time when, to quote William Butler Yeats, "the centre cannot hold," being adrift is terrifying.[1] In the face of bewildering change and even chaos, people want to feel they matter.

While purpose has a few different dimensions—spiritual, familial, professional—it's the one that we're concerned about here. We need to understand who we are and in what context we are supposed to do work. More important, we want to know what our work *is*. What we find ourselves looking for is what Vicktor Frankl wrote about in *Man's Search For Meaning* shortly after World War II—that people are driven to figure out what they were put on this planet to do and to be.[2]

Time after time, students show up in my office as they begin their journey here at the Harvard Business School. They see nine hundred other new MBAs looking for answers and struggling with whether they have chosen the right career or whether they need to find a new career path. They wonder if they are anything other than their résumé. In the process of reflection they begin to ask more fundamental questions centered on their relationship with self, personal relationships, their family of origin, their values, motives, and needs.[3] Many are figuring out their own self-perceived talents and, more important, those career drives that guide and direct their career decisions.[4] Many have had relatively few career experiences and want assurances that they have made the right choices and are heading in the right direction.

All this relates to purpose—these students want to find meaning in and through work. To many, what's meaningful has to do with status. More specifically, they want to work for companies or in professions or on tasks that carry with them a certain amount of prestige. One student said that he liked telling people he worked for Disney because everyone thought how great it would be to work for a place that focuses on bringing happiness. Others wanted to work for Procter & Gamble because P&G represented prestige in the consumer products world. This is referent prestige, and it derives from being associated with a company that has created a strong brand. In the same vein, though our students often express humility about being in the Harvard MBA program, they seem to be proud to be associated with the School.

How we see ourselves, though, goes beyond the status conferred by a job or organization. The deeper psychological issue relates to our self-concept. Our identity has to do with how we tell the story about ourselves. This is worth repeating. What is important is not necessarily the actual story about ourselves but the story we tell ourselves about our personal journey. If we have had a terrible work experience, do we see ourselves as failures or as learners who benefit from difficult but knowledge-enhancing events? These cumulative experiences shape us as we seek our purpose. Obviously, we don't want to put such a positive spin on our stories that they come out deceptive or self-delusional. We can, however, look at our experience and tell stories that focus on learning, growth, and development so that we leverage our past rather than becoming enslaved by it. Through these stories, we seek a definition of purpose, of who we are in relationship to others and to our life experiences.

Many of us tell our stories in a way that reflects our anxieties. The less clarity we have around our direction and purpose, the more anxiety we have. This is true for young and old, for young professionals and CEOs. You would think that those who have achieved a certain stature appropriate to their age might not be burdened with these anxieties— but you'd be wrong. For instance, the young men and women in the Harvard MBA program are in the educational elite, yet a significant percentage of them are very anxious, as their storytelling suggests. These twenty-somethings relate tales that indicate they're self-critical over the fact that they don't know exactly what they should be doing with their careers. Juan, a twenty-seven-year-old student, called to ask for an appointment. He told my assistant that he wanted guidance on his life and the direction he should take. When we met, he said, "Professor DeLong, you seem so passionate about what you do. You seem satisfied with your career. I want to be that satisfied. How do I get from where I am as a very confused MBA student to someone who is absolutely clear about his direction and intentions?"

I answered, "I was forty-six before I knew that my talents and my current job fit my purpose, where there was complete alignment." Regardless, I could see that he was still beating himself up for not finding his path. As a highly ambitious, driven young man, Juan was almost desperate to find his purpose and find it fast. Humans are goal seekers, and high-need-for-achievement professionals are driven to seek ambitious goals. Whether they're just starting out like Juan or are in the middle of their careers, they thrive best when purpose is at the center of their activities. When they are not sure where to go or why they should go in a particular direction or, most important, why they are even doing what they're doing, self-doubt and fundamental questions about life and its essence ensue. Or, in terms of the triangle image (figure 2-1), anxiety increases and overwhelms.

Sanjay left a prestigious job when the CEO who hired him stepped aside. Rather than take the first big role that was offered to him, he decided that he should take some time to reflect on whether he wanted to teach at a university, consult, or take on another major role before he retired. After a few months passed, he became increasingly worried about whether he would ever find the right next step. He also was concerned that no one would hire someone in midcareer.

One evening I received a call from Sanjay. He said, "The longer I have time to think about life and work and family the more I worry about the most basic issues of life. I realize that perhaps it's just better to take any job so I don't have to think about more fundamental questions like, 'What's my real purpose in life?' Am I just filling my time being busy so I don't have to think about these questions? I guess what I'm realizing is that I need purpose in life and in my work and if I don't [have it], the anxiety and worry becomes almost insurmountable."

People become anxious about their direction not only when they're between jobs but when they're working. Being employed doesn't guarantee a free pass from anxiety. In fact, many well-paid professionals at prestigious organizations are beset by anxiety because they've lost a sense of purpose. In *When Professionals Have to Lead,* a book I coauthored with John J. Gabarro and Robert J. Lees, we outlined a leadership model that is a guide for those who are in fields like financial services, consulting, medicine, universities, and accountancy.[5] These careers are usually defined by partnerships and are structured as three-tiered stratified apprenticeships. In this leadership model, the first responsibility for the leader is to create direction for the professionals in the organization. We know that those professionals need a picture of the future; that they are so focused on the task at hand that they require an authoritative voice to place their work in a larger context. When these hard-driving professionals are physically removed from headquarters, as is often the case, they need to feel connected and moving in harmony with their colleagues. In this way, they find purpose and rein in their anxieties.

Think about whether you feel like your work is connected to a larger purpose. If you work for an organization, ask yourself:

- Do I understand how my work is important?

- Does my boss do a good job of showing me how my assignments connect to larger organizational goals?

- Do I feel like I'm just doing tasks or do I grasp how these tasks are pieces of a larger whole?

If you work for yourself or run a business, ask yourself:

- Am I working just for the money or do I believe that what I'm doing has a larger significance?

- Do I derive satisfaction from knowing that my efforts provide work for others?

- Do I feel that I'm making a significant contribution to my organization? That I am using my knowledge and skills in ways that really matter to me as a person and to the success of the organization?

The Nuances of Purpose

When people have a clear sense of purpose, anxiety usually doesn't get in the way of accomplishment. We have examples throughout history of groups that have accomplished ambitious goals despite obstacles and setbacks. Charles O'Reilly and Michael Tushman write eloquently about ordinary people who do extraordinary things by finding direction through purpose.[6] Remain in jail for twenty-seven years and then lead your country out of apartheid. Cross the plains of the United States in the dead of winter in covered wagons so you can worship God as you wish. Be the first country to land a man on the moon. Bring down a wall that divided a country.

Purpose, therefore, can help high-need-for-achievement professionals clear a path through the anxiety toward achieving their ambitious goals. Achieving purpose, however, can be challenging for people today. For one thing, their organizations are not always smart about providing direction, communicating larger company goals, or helping their people find meaningful, satisfying work. For another thing, the nature of that work is changing, forcing people to question their purpose and causing them to become confused about it; the attorney who relished using his legal skills and knowledge is now being asked to bring in business; the doctor who loved her job is now being challenged by bottom-line-driven administrations on one front and insurance companies on another. In addition, purpose changes with time, and what was satisfying then might not be satisfying now; the hard-charging business executive who wanted only to make partner finds that being partner isn't enough and requires a new and more ambitious raison d'être.

It's possible that you never framed your dissatisfaction with your career or your disappointment in your achievements in terms of purpose. You may have rued bad job choices or changes in your industry or company, but you never formally asked yourself, "Why am I doing what I'm doing?" This is completely understandable—we tend to become focused on our here-and-now daily tasks rather than the larger question of purpose. Later in the book, we will focus more on why we fill our agendas with busy work so we don't have to ask tougher, reflective questions. Yet this larger issue of purpose is always in the back of our minds, especially if we're high-need-for-achievement professionals. We want to feel what we do matters. We want to believe that we're making a difference. If we feel we're just "doing a job," it doesn't matter how well we're doing it. Without purpose, we allow anxiety to creep in, and that anxiety makes it difficult, if impossible, to find the achievement and satisfaction we seek.

It helps, therefore, to identify if purpose is lacking from your work. I just noted four reasons it might be lacking—organizational failures, changing work environment, changing personal requirements, and lack of self-awareness. Let's look at each cause, decide whether it applies to you, and learn what you can do about it.

Organizational Failures

Many organizations want to give their people a sense of direction and purpose, but scores of obstacles prevent them from doing so. They may have a program in place designed to communicate to key people throughout the company how and why their work matters, but that program may become lost amid the deadline pressures and occasional crises that crop up. The CEO may espouse the need for employees to understand the significance of their contributions, yet the organization doesn't reward this behavior, so executives aren't motivated to help their people find their purpose.

The disconnect between organizational intentions and actions, though, is probably the most significant reason you find yourself without a clear sense of why you're working (and why you're working so hard!). Chris Argyris studied why certain leaders in organizations say one thing and do another.[7] To illustrate that point, he recalled how, during World War II, he led a team at a shipbuilding site in Chicago, and the team threw him a party when he was reassigned to Brooklyn Yards. Years later, when he visited his team back on the shores of Lake Michigan, he asked his workers what they really thought of him as a leader. Worker after worker told him that he was terrible, the worst team leader they had had. Arygris asked why they had thrown a party for him when he left. They told him almost in unison that it was because they were thrilled that he was leaving. It was a celebration of sorts.

Over the years Argyris refined a model that highlights the destructive nature of organizations and leaders within them that have what he calls an espoused theory (what the organization purports is its purpose) and the theory in use (what actually happens in the organization, how things get done, how people are really treated, and so forth). Argyris' work team noted that he would say that he was open to discuss different work processes, but they didn't experience him as being open at all. He said he would be supportive of new ideas, but experience told them otherwise. The difference between what we say and how others experience what we do causes pain for employees.

They expect one thing and get another. The greater the dissonance we create, the greater the pain, frustration, and anger that others feel.

Think about whether you're experiencing a similar disconnect in your workplace between what a leader says and does. If so, your boss or other executives may have communicated the importance of your contributions, but you distrust what they've told you because their actions contradict what they've communicated. For instance, they've insisted that your ability to run idea-generating, cross-functional teams is crucial, yet you see others being rewarded with promotions and bigger bonuses for other types of contributions. Why, then, are you breaking your back in keeping this team up and running? Is your purpose valid or is it just window dressing for an organization that wants to say it has this type of team?

If you are struggling with your purpose because of this organizational disconnect, you probably exhibit the following two qualities:

- Cynicism: You are frequently skeptical when your bosses give you assignments or tell you how important these assignments are to the organization; you tell others that your bosses have hidden agendas when they launch new projects and programs.

- Lack of identity: You no longer know who you are within the context of your organization; you cannot clearly articulate the role you play and how that role contributes to your group's and organization's success; you perceive a disconnect between how you see yourself and how the organization views you.

In these situations, you have a few choices for regaining a clear sense of purpose. Restructure your job so that your tasks and ways of working are more aligned with your own sense of your professional self. You may be able to restructure the job on your own, or you may need to sit down and talk with your boss about it. Sometimes people add new responsibilities in order to feel more connected to their purpose—by volunteering for a cross-functional team or by loaning themselves out to another group that they feel is doing what they should be doing. In other instances, they need to make more dramatic shifts—transferring to another group, taking a new job, or even going back to school or retraining themselves for a significantly different type of work.

Changing Work Environment

Think about how excited you were when you landed a job, received your first managerial position, or started your own business. At the moment, your purpose was clear. You knew why you were working and received tremendous satisfaction from what you did. You defined yourself as a company person, as a manager, or as a business owner. You knew what you were doing, why you were doing it, and where you were heading. It was a highly purposeful existence.

But things changed.

Consider Bob, who joined a law firm in the 1980s when selling client work wasn't required; the business flew in the door. As more and more companies relied on internal legal departments to do legal work and competition intensified, though, the larger firms, especially, began to expect all partners to bring in new clients.

Unsure how to do this, Bob felt increasingly obsolete. Senior management became increasingly critical, and their negative feedback reinforced Bob's sense of inadequacy. The simple fact was that Bob didn't know how to sell business. His purpose was to use his extensive and deep legal expertise to the best of his ability—this is what he had always done and what had brought him and his clients satisfaction. Now, though, Bob felt like the bar of various internal metrics had shifted dramatically higher, right before his eyes. Now, rather than being seen as a solid contributing partner, he was viewed as someone who didn't carry his weight. Some of the younger, more ambitious professionals perceived him as overhead, bringing down the partner-to-professional ratios on which compensation was based. Every day Bob felt less and less like a contributor to the purpose of the organization.

Bob's firm certainly could have handled this situation better. After all, his legal expertise was invaluable, and the firm could have either made it clear he was valued for this expertise or helped him reassess his role in a more positive way. Unfortunately, leaders in organizations sometimes fail to recognize the value of purpose in their professionals' work lives.

Therefore, it's up to you to respond to events and situations that cause you to be confused about your purpose. This means being aware of how shifting events in your field or company have impacted the way you define yourself. While it seems obvious that someone like Bob should have recognized that events beyond his control had created the problems he faced, this recognition is difficult in the heat of the moment. Instead, we become anxious as we find that we're no longer valued as we once were, and this anxiety causes us to retreat into our shells, to continue to try and do the wrong thing well.

Raise your awareness of events that are causing you to feel devalued by asking the following questions:

- What industry trends are affecting my value to my company or my customers?

- What shifts within my organization are rendering me less effective or less productive than in the past?

- At the peak of my success during the last ten years, what skill or type of knowledge (or combination thereof) singled me out as a high performer? Has that skill or knowledge been devalued in any way by events inside or outside of my organization?

- Do I feel out of synch with where the organization is headed?

What might Bob's firm have done differently? What might Bob have done differently? These are two big questions that will be answered more fully in ensuing chapters. For now, though, recognize that Bob's firm failed to clarify the firm's new direction and provide Bob with a clear sense of his place in this evolving law practice; they also didn't give him the coaching or development he needed or engage him in conversations to help him understand his role in the changing firm. For his part, Bob became trapped by his anxieties over his diminishing role; he took the negative attitudes of younger lawyers and partners to heart, locking himself into his work routines and preventing himself from trying to do the right thing poorly.

Changing Personal Requirements

In other words, you've changed. You may have started out driven to make partner in a consulting firm but now you're obsessed with making a go of your own business. Or, when you were younger, your purpose may have been to make a difference in the world through your work. Now that you're older and have a family to support, your purpose has shifted—you want to achieve a measure of financial success and job stability.

Changes can be less dramatic but no less significant. You may derive greater satisfaction from developing your people at this stage of your career than individual accomplishment. You may have a particular long-range project or goal that is consuming your attention. You may have changed jobs, experienced a life event (divorce, birth of a child, death of someone close to you) that has impacted what you believe your purpose to be.

When your purpose shifts, whether in major or minor ways, you may find yourself beset by anxiety. When this happens, though, you probably aren't cognizant that the changes going on in your life have made it necessary for you to think about a different purpose. Instead, you just find yourself becoming more dissatisfied with your job or more worried about the work you're doing. Because of this lack of awareness, you don't realize you need to talk to someone about what's missing in your professional life. You don't understand that to achieve all the goals that flow from your new purpose, you may have to transfer to another group or even change jobs.

Have personal changes impacted your purpose? To answer that question, try thinking about these questions:

- If you were to compare what you were driven to achieve at work five or ten years ago versus today, has anything changed?

- Do you feel that what you enjoy doing at work—the skills and knowledge you relish using—have changed, whether in obvious or subtle ways?

- Is the story you tell yourself about yourself as a professional different now than it was in the past? Have changes in your personal life or in your work interests and situation changed in ways that you're no longer the same professional as you were in the past?

Facilitate Your Pursuit of Purpose

If lack of purpose is a problem in your work life, if it is causing you sleepless nights and anxiety-filled days, and is preventing you from moving from the left to the right side of the 2 × 2 matrix, then you need to take action. Awareness of this state is an excellent first step, and my previous suggestions should help you in that regard. But consider two other options that can get you past your anxiety and help you muster the courage to change and grow aligned with your purpose:

- Seek full engagement with your work.

- Demand straight talk rather than ambiguity.

Seek Full Engagement with Your Work

Many highly ambitious, fast-track professionals become disengaged or only partially engaged with their jobs. They do perfectly competent work, but they lack the commitment and belief in what they're doing that emboldens them to take risks, accept new challenges, and produce at the highest levels.

To engage fully, you may need to make adjustments in how or even where you work. What's required may be something as simple as an honest, open discussion with your boss, one in which you communicate what you feel is missing and what your boss might do to supply that missing piece. You may need clarification of your role and how it fits into the larger organization, or you may need a fresh assignment that makes you feel as though you are using your abilities to their fullest. At the other extreme, you may need to change jobs within the company or without in order to feel engaged fully in your work.

Engagement isn't a given. It doesn't just happen. You need to take responsibility for making adjustments so that you can again work purposefully; you can't expect organizations to do it for you. I recognize that finding purposeful work can take time and effort, but it's worth it. A variety of studies indicate that people who are more committed to the organization and its direction are more likely to be high performers. In fact, a high correlation exists between the highest performers and those who are most engaged with the organization. It's not just that they work the hardest, but that their purposeful engagement helps them take risks, adapt their behaviors to situations, and motivate them to do the right thing poorly; they know that it's worth the sacrifice of not appearing invulnerable for a brief period of time in order to master a critical new skill or area of knowledge. I've interviewed a number of high-need-for-achievement performers who demonstrated this engagement; to convey this engaged mind-set, here's what one of these people had to say: "I've had a lot of jobs and bosses and opportunities to be committed to other people and other companies. I've never experienced anything like I have here. There is a clarity of purpose that we all share from top to bottom. That clarity shows up in how I spend my time, how I work with my colleagues, how I get feedback from my boss, how the leaders of the organization treat people inside and outside the organization. I've never confessed that I would actually work for less to experience what I'm experiencing here. Sometimes I find myself late at night working on a project with colleagues. I'm away from family. I'm eating cold, very ordinary Chinese food in a room that is too hot with no ventilation. And I find myself saying to myself, 'I'm loving being here with these people working for these clients even at this time of night. This is craziness and I love it.'"

Have you achieved this type of full engagement? You don't have to reach the almost messianic fervor of this interviewee, but you should possess a strong belief in your work, how you're doing it, and where you're doing it. More specifically, here are the criteria for full engagement:

- A feeling that the values of the place you work are aligned with your values

- A feeling that senior management are aligned with one another

- Some clarity that your daily tasks are leading you in the career direction in which you want to go

- A belief in the work you do—an inner sense that this work represents your calling

- Recognition that your skills and knowledge are being used wisely

- A lack of dissonance between your work expectations and your work realities

Demand Straight Talk Rather Than Ambiguity

During World War II Winston Churchill was marking up a classified document that the Allied Forces generals were waiting for in order to go into action. On one of the pages Churchill wrote, "Watch the borders," referring to the manner in which the typist had left little room for him to make comments in the margins. When the generals read the document they believed that they were being advised by Churchill to watch the English borders in southeast England in order to stop a possible invasion by the enemy. Luckily, there was no invasion. Luckily, thousands weren't killed because of a misunderstanding between Churchill and his generals and the typist.

High-need-for-achievement professionals need clarity, not ambiguity. When bosses, customers, or others fail to make their meaning clear, they ratchet up anxieties. You turn in a project to your boss and when you ask what he thought of it, he gives you nothing more than a nod. Did he feel you let him down? Is he so displeased that he is deliberately holding his tongue for fear of devastating you? Does his nod signify it was just okay, far below what he expected of you?

Driven, ambitious people generally assume the worst about ambiguous responses. If there are repeated ambiguities, they turn their negative feelings inward and start creating worst-case scenarios; they begin to question their purpose of working at the company. Maybe, with all the changes that have been going on, they no longer belong there. Maybe they have overstayed their welcome and are viewed by others as over-the-hill. Ambiguity provides a fertile field for anxieties to thrive.

You have every right to expect even your largest customers and most powerful bosses to communicate with you unambiguously. Too many of us don't. We don't ask for clarification because we fear what we might hear. We don't want to discover that the nod we received was in fact a nod of disappointment. Yet it's better to hear the truth than to allow anxieties to surface in the wake of ambiguity. And in most instances, clarity will provide reassurance, since most people who are ambiguous don't even realize that they're being ambiguous. And even negative feedback can be reassuring because you know where you stand and what you need to work on.

I certainly was unaware when I committed this mistake. If I had been more aware, I would have caused less frustration and anger with others around me. One day at the end of one of my MBA classes, I began to rush out of the room, walking briskly past students to set up to teach another class. The class had gone well in my mind. The students seemed to have been highly engaged in the case, which was one of my favorites. I knew that students connected with it whenever I taught it. As I hurried up toward the exit a student looked up at me and said, "Professor DeLong, that was really a good class and discussion." I paused for a moment and looked at him. I think I gave him a bit of a blank stare. I didn't respond verbally but quickly moved on out the door. I had only ten minutes to get to my next class and get organized to teach another ninety students. I also had to speak with a student who had had some health problems and wanted to check in with me. I also knew that there would be some parents visiting class from out of the country.

What kind of thoughts and feelings and emotions did I generate for this student who complimented me on my way out the door? I'm not sure why I didn't say something. But given the situation, I was surprised when this student (let's call him Bruce) set up an appointment to talk with me in my office in five days. By the time we met, I had noticed that Bruce hadn't participated in any of the classes after the incident. At our meeting I asked Bruce how it was going and tried to make small talk before we moved on to his agenda for meeting.

Bruce began the conversation by asking me how he was doing in class and whether I valued his comments. I told him he was doing fine so far at the midway point of the class. He asked whether there was something he did that put me off or angered me. I wondered why he was asking. He then played back to me the incident that had occurred at the end of class just five days earlier. He said after I walked out he began to think that there must have been something wrong with what he had said. Perhaps I didn't hear him. Perhaps I thought I was too important (he mentioned this only later in our relationship) to respond. He began to dwell on the comment he had made that day in class and assumed I didn't like it. He then began to review his performance to date in class and wondered how he was doing. Each time he asked me one of these questions he responded in the negative. Worry set in, and he manufactured more negative possibilities than even a poor student might produce (and he was far from a poor student). By the time Bruce and I sat down to talk, he was a nervous wreck.

I admitted that I should have handled the situation differently and told him I was in a hurry when I didn't respond. I added that he had interpreted the interaction negatively; he had misread my response. When he realized all the things I had on my mind he was surprised. I told him that I was focused only on getting to the next class and taking care of the administrative stuff before class began again for the second class.

When I was thirty years old I found myself at a ball game at the old Memorial Coliseum in Portland with my father. While we watched the Portland Trailblazers play the Houston Rockets, I asked him about some of his experiences balancing raising five children with his professional career. I remember asking him, "Dad, why were you often in such a bad mood during the ten years before I headed off to college?"

He asked what I was talking about. I said, "You know, when you would come home from work you were so quiet at the dinner table. On many occasions you were curt with us. All of us thought we had done something wrong or that we were in trouble. After dinner you would head for the couch and fall asleep while reading the paper. For a long period of time during those growing-up years we thought you were mad at us." He replied, "Nothing could be further from the truth. The fact is I was worried about the business. I was worried about meeting all the demands that I felt every day. I know on occasion I would get short with you and your brothers and sister. But in general I was pleased with all you kids. I know you had the normal challenges growing up but I wasn't angry in general. You just misread me."

Given our reflex to misread ambiguous communications, ask for clarity in the following ways:

- Express your uncertainty: Tell the ambiguous communicator that you don't understand what he means by his nod or his neutral statement. Say something like, "I'm sorry, but I can't figure out what you're trying to tell me by . . ."

- Express your concern: Address the biggest fear you're reading into the ambiguous communication. Don't beat around the bush. Say, "Does this mean I'm in trouble?" In most instances, your fears are unfounded and when the other person demonstrates this fact, it will lessen your anxiety.

The Right Path: Assess Where You've Been, Where You Are, and Where You're Heading

By engaging fully and demanding straight talk, you increase the odds of working with a purpose. This is absolutely essential if you're to make the courageous journey from one quadrant to the next, from doing the wrong thing well to doing the right thing poorly to doing the right thing well. Think of purpose as a necessary vehicle for this journey. It provides power and direction when you hit rough patches. As you try new things and have to adjust how you work, it keeps you moving through the two-by-two matrix. As I've noted, many high-need-for-achievement professionals become stuck at some point in their careers, and purpose is what prevents this from happening—or it helps you get out of your rut.

High-need-for-achievement individuals think about a lot of things—how their careers compare to others, whether they're being rewarded fairly for their work, how close they are to reaching a career goal—but they often don't dwell on their purpose. For some, it seems too esoteric a concept, too removed from their laser focus on achievement in the here-and-now. I would urge you, however, to think about your purpose regularly. Reflect on what it was when you started out, what it is now, and what you hope to do in the future.

Don't worry if your purpose isn't a grandiose statement like, "I want to make a difference in the world" (though it's great if it is). Purpose can take an infinite variety of forms and be articulated in an equally endless number of ways. Your purpose may be to do good work for the leading company in your industry. It may be that you want to be the type of leader who grows both his people and the business. It may be that you want to feel valued and that you're making a contribution regardless of significance.

Whatever it is, think about it often and hold it close. It will help you keep moving forward and prevent you from being derailed by the anxiety that arises during different stages of your journey.

CHAPTER FOUR

Isolation

Why Do I Keep Voting Myself Off the Island?

HIGH-NEED-FOR-ACHIEVEMENT PROFESSIONALS want to believe they're in the inner circle, that they're members of the club. Successful, smart professionals may seem sufficiently confident that they don't need this sense of inclusion, but beneath that outer confidence is an inner doubter: Do I measure up? Am I as good as everyone thinks I am? Does management see me as an indispensable A player or as a disposable part? These questions plague even some of the most successful professionals. When they can't answer them affirmatively, they become anxious. They fret that they've fallen from favor or off the fast track. They begin to see themselves on the outside looking in, and they become concerned.

It doesn't matter if their perceptions are inaccurate. Management may love them, but in their own minds, they feel they've been excluded. In this instance, perception is reality. As long as they believe that they've been cast out, they behave in ways that will hamper their performance and their sense of fulfillment. In fact, even if they weren't excluded to begin with, their anxieties will ensure that their productivity will suffer, and soon they will ensure that they're on the outs with management.

This feeling of isolation can develop in various ways, sometimes obvious and sometimes subtle. Many high achievers are particularly sensitive to exclusionary behaviors. Are you? Does this sound like the story of your life in recent years? Before answering, consider the story of a highly driven professional who perceived that he was on the outside looking in.

Rob Parson cared deeply about his boss, Paul Nasr. He had followed Nasr on Wall Street, moving to two different firms based on the relationship. Paul Nasr was a gifted client guy. He didn't just sell firm products but created specific and unique products based on genuine client needs. In the early '90s when he received a special invitation from John Mack, then president of Morgan Stanley, Nasr jumped at the chance to be led by Mack. The first person Nasr brought along with him from his previous firm was Rob Parson. They trusted each other to the extent that they could finish each other's sentences. One glance during a client meeting was all it took for them to be on the same page. They dined together, drank together, and shared common concerns specific to the world of Wall Street.

One of the reasons Parson moved to Morgan Stanley was that he had always wanted to prove to himself and others that he could join the elite of Wall Street. Goldman Sachs and Morgan Stanley were seen as the two premier institutions at the time, offering the promise of status, worldwide recognition, and opportunities for financial rewards.

Most important, Ivy League graduates staffed headquarters, and they seemed never to have suffered or been knocked down by people they feared.

At the time, the policy was that no one from another firm could join Morgan Stanley as a managing director. Newcomers needed to join as executive directors and work their way up. So Rob Parson moved from managing director in his old firm to principal at Morgan Stanley, with the understanding that if he transformed the business he would be promoted in eleven months when the promotion and compensation lists were announced.

Before Rob Parson took on the task of building a business that was tenth in the ranking and had 2 percent market share, five other managing directors, all with guaranteed contracts, had attempted to do the same. Each left the firm after a year of failure and embarrassment. Each of these leaders was paid over $1 million in salary. The executive directors, vice presidents, and associates in the group were demoralized when Parson took over. They felt that they were not learning the business or using any of their talents. They felt they were falling behind their friends in other firms who were moving up through the ranks. And they were not getting paid what they had dreamed they would be compensated. Basically, they were depressed and angry and frightened as they ruminated about their careers.

Parson began to do his magic in client development and service. He would take junior professionals with him and pull rabbits out of a hat, creating outstanding work for the firm and the professionals themselves. And he was a walking volcano. At any time he could erupt and yell and use language that would make a sailor proud. He could blow up at an airport, in a restaurant, or in the office. If Parson felt that an employee was not thinking strategically, or listening and learning fast enough, he would make it known in no uncertain terms and in front of other professionals. The irony was that he exhibited the opposite behaviors with clients. They loved him. He listened, he cajoled, he made friends with them immediately. They called weeks in advance to find a place on his calendar. They called him for personal advice.

The business began to grow. And it grew fast and efficiently, and everyone at Morgan Stanley and on Wall Street watched Parson transform it. The person who watched the most closely was Paul Nasr. Before Parson arrived, Nasr saw the rankings in free fall. Then he witnessed their market share climb to 12.2 percent in less than eleven months under Parson's leadership. While Nasr heard stories that Parson was tough on his people, he did little about it. On occasion he would tease Parson about lightening up a bit. But he never actually confronted him about how his behavior was counter to the kind of place Morgan Stanley leadership wanted to create. Nor did anyone from human resources check in with Parson or Nasr to discuss how things were going.

When it was time for Parson to be reviewed for promotion, Nasr sent his promotion packet to the promotion committee. The head of the committee worried about what he heard about Parson on both the positive and negative sides of the ledger. When he briefly discussed it with John Mack, they both agreed that he would not make the performance bar for promotion when the list was posted. When Nasr came to Mack's office to ask what Mack thought about promotion possibilities, Mack said Parson wouldn't be promoted. After a brief conversation Nasr left the room and headed for his office on the trading floor. As he walked to the elevator, every conceivable thought raced through his head. *Do I quit? What and when do I tell Rob? How should I tell him? I've let him down. My career is now ruined because Mack thinks I can't manage. What if Rob quits? What will happen with market share? Who can replace him? What will happen to my bonus if he leaves? If Rob leaves will clients go with him?*

Nasr decided to tell Parson that day, one month before the official promotion and compensation list would be posted. He wanted to get the conversation over with. Nasr invited Parson for drinks after work. After a number of drinks Nasr turned to Parson and said, "By the way, you aren't getting promoted." Parson stared at him for a few moments and then yelled a few obscenities and walked out of the bar.

Parson didn't come to work the next day. At about 6:00 p.m. on that day Parson contacted the head of the promotion committee; he wanted to talk. They met that night and chatted for a couple of hours. Parson reflected, "I spent the last twenty-four hours looking at my résumé. I've been contacted by most of the Wall Street firms to leave for twice the money. Yet I've moved around so much. And on some level I really believe that Mack wants to create the best firm on Wall Street. I believe him. So I want to discuss an alternative. I've decided that I will stay at Morgan Stanley on one condition. And that is that I never have to report to Paul Nasr again. In fact, I never want to see him again. He lied to me. I trusted him absolutely, and once again I'm looking inside the firm and at a select group of people who have rejected me. I wanted to be a managing director more than anything else. And once again I'm outside looking in. Once again, I didn't make it into the club. And Nasr abandoned me at the last minute."

Rob Parson bet his career on being promoted to managing director at Morgan Stanley. Because he didn't go to a prestigious school and lacked a privileged background, he thought of himself as less sophisticated than many of his colleagues. Every day when he entered the headquarters at 1585 Broadway, he compared himself to others and felt on some deeper level that he came up short; he suspected that he wasn't quite worthy of being a member of this esteemed group. And as he reflected later, "I think I was on the margin angry most of the time. I now realize that I had a chip on my shoulder and dared the world to try and knock it off. I also realized that for the most part I never felt included in the club."

I've spent so much time relating this story because it demonstrates how exclusion can take place in myriad ways. At the end of the story,

Parson was literally excluded from the promotion club. Even before that, he had had a pervasive sense of exclusion because he lacked the same social pedigree as many of his colleagues. Ironically, his angry behaviors, caused by that sense of exclusion, resulted in his being turned down for promotion. When Parson was brought into Morgan Stanley, members of his group felt excluded because he, rather than one of them, had been chosen for this leadership position.

It's not just the people at Morgan Stanley who have this fear of disconnection but professionals everywhere. The fundamental questions that individuals ask as they stand on the edge of a group are: "Am I in or out? Am I a member of the club or not? Will I ever fit into this group or team or division or organization?" Certainly, some people are firmly ensconced in their organization's inner circle and feel secure. The majority, however, feel like they are drifting towards the outer edges of the circle. At that point, they begin to act differently, abnormally. They begin to look over their shoulder and worry. Their behavior changes, which further isolates them. Caught in this vicious cycle, people find themselves moving from thinking they're being excluded, to drifting toward the outer edges of the circle, to being exiled.

Are you caught in this vicious cycle? How aware are you of feelings of isolation and exclusion, and do they make you anxious? Many high-need-for-achievement professionals aren't aware that this is happening, in part because it's a tough thing for some driven individuals to recognize. They work hard and put up a tough front, unable to admit to themselves that they feel overlooked or ignored.

To maintain awareness of the degree of isolation you experience, reflect on the following questions:

- Do you sometimes feel as if you're different from or "less than" your colleagues? That you're younger or older than they are, come from a different corporate culture, lack their background and knowledge, etc?

- Despite your success, do you believe that your boss favors others over you? Does it seem that no matter what you do or how well you do it, there's always someone else who is favored?

- Do you find yourself worried that you don't fit in with your company or culture? Do you spend a lot of time agonizing over what you can do to fit in better?

- When you're passed over for a promotion or not given an assignment you believe you should have received, do you find yourself dwelling on what you think of as "a snub"? Do you obsess about why you didn't get what you wanted, even when it's possible that you weren't ready for the promotion or someone else was better suited to the assignment?

The Relationship Between
Commitment and Isolation

Commitment is essential for connection. Unfortunately, if you're like most people, you may realize that a variety of environmental factors may have diminished your commitment to your work and your organization. Consciously or not, you've disconnected. This may have happened because you feel you've been excluded, as in our earlier examples. It may also occur because your company had downsized and demoralized you to the point that it's difficult to feel any sense of loyalty to the leaders of the firm. Whatever the reason, you no longer are as committed as you once were to your career, your company, your specific job and the tasks that come with it. Without this commitment, you feel isolated and alone. Whether this isolation is real or imagined doesn't matter. It produces anxiety that makes you unwilling to try something new, to change how you work, to have the courage to do the right thing poorly.

Some of you may be fortunate enough to have found employment where inclusion is a core value. In these cases, you probably feel a strong sense of commitment to your work and connection to the organization's goals and values. For instance, at consulting firm McKinsey & Company, many high-need-for-achievement professionals transcend their anxiety. That's because McKinsey makes inclusion its mission. One former director stated, "As much as I would like to find something bad to say about McKinsey, my experience was positive. More important, the way they treated me when I decided to leave made me feel proud to be a part of this group of professionals. I always felt included even after I left." This particular partner had been with the firm over fifteen years, so you may think that his seniority had a lot to do with the positive way in which he was treated. In fact, people who stay with the firm for only two or three years say essentially the same things upon leaving.

McKinsey spends more money per professional assisting exiting professionals than any other firm. It allows people to stay for up to six months with pay. It continues to make these people feel part of the team even though they have made other career decisions. Career coaching is part of the process for everyone at all levels. The firm even shares its networking capabilities with exiting employees. Even more surprising, once professionals exit McKinsey, communication increases between them and the firm. McKinsey believes that everyone who leaves the organization is either going to be a future client or a consultant who might refer work to or cheerlead for the organization.

My point here is that your sense of commitment to a company is likely to increase when a company demonstrates that it is committed to you.

In some situations, however, your sense of commitment is less determined by the company you work for and more impacted by your own internal dreams and demons. High-need-for-achievement personalities can fool themselves about how connected they are, telling themselves and others that they are fiercely loyal to their companies and their work. They are afraid to admit the truth that they no longer feel in touch with their skills or their evolving organizational cultures. They can experience anomie even when they work for vibrant organizations like McKinsey—something inside of them is making them feel isolated, even though their culture, their boss, and their colleagues are trying to make them feel involved.

To understand your connection—and your disconnection—to work on a deeper level, consider the concept of career anchors, introduced by Edgar Schein in the late '70s. These anchors consist of values, motives, and needs that constitute a way we experience the world of work. Schein asserts that certain motivational, talent, and value self-images, formed through work experience, function to guide and constrain our entire careers. These self-images act, in effect, as career anchors that not only influence career choices but also affect decisions to move from one employer to another, shape what individuals are looking for in life, and color their views of the future.[1]

In essence, we feel anchored to the work we do or the company we work for based on a mix of factors. To help you determine how anchored you are to your job, let's look at three dimensions that determine whether you feel connected or isolated:

- Technical competence

- Hierarchical journey

- Boundary of inclusion

Technical Competence

The first dimension is knowledge/skills, a sense of technical, functional competence. When you begin your career, you must focus on being technically proficient. This is the ante that gets you into the team, group, and organizational game. As you gain proficiency, you gain acceptance and forge bonds with the larger group that are both external and internal. Externally, you are given more roles and responsibilities as your technical expertise increases. Internally, you feel like you belong because of the competency you demonstrate and the rewards you receive. Conversely, when you fail to learn a new skill or demonstrate competence in some area, you feel like a failure. More to the point, you have the sense that the people who used to like and accept you now view you as less smart, less effective, less promotable. You believe that because you failed to master a competency, you are no longer on the fast track or even a member of the club.

Learning takes place on multiple levels. As a new associate in a law firm, you must not only learn the law but also how to navigate in the system. You need to learn how to work with others, how to support them and be supported. You need to learn how to work without hand-holding or feedback from others. You need to build a reputation for being competent in a particular part of the law such as tax, litigation, or real estate. You actually build a career reputation and self-concept based on your technical skills (see figure 4–1).

Hierarchical Journey

The second dimension that you must manage is the hierarchical journey up the organization ladder. These vertical ladders stand in front of people as they enter all systems, whether as children entering school or professors starting a job. They are intertwined with our biosocial stages along with our familial stages. When you receive promotions as well as assignments of increasingly greater responsibility, you feel included. On the other hand, if you fall off and think you are behind, you begin to feel exposed and frightened that you are losing the race. You begin to question your abilities.

Anxiety really takes hold in this dimension, since when you don't receive a promotion or key assignment and others do, you possess

FIGURE 4-1

Three career dimensions

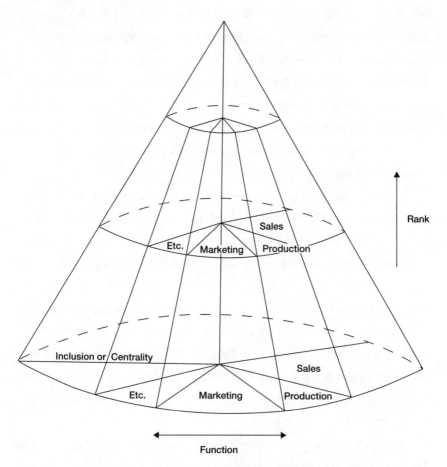

Source: Edgar H. Schein, *Career Anchors: Discovering Your Real Values* (San Diego, CA: Pfeiffer & Company, 1993), 17.

tangible "proof" that you have been excluded. You worry whether someone is moving more rapidly than you. You worry whether someone else is spending more time with the movers and shakers of the organization. And you worry about whether you are on schedule to make it to the next organizational level or benchmark.

Ashish Nanda, a professor at the Harvard Law School, wrote a case about a young and ambitious lawyer who had met all the hierarchical benchmarks. He was asked to take an international assignment in Hong Kong. After his time away from London headquarters he returned five years later to observe that he had fallen behind colleagues who had moved very fast through their organization. He noticed that the values of the firm had changed since he was gone: partners now focused primarily on their own silos and their own business. After achieving partner, he received news that he had been passed over to become a new department head in the firm.

Someone younger had been selected. The writing for this individual was on the wall. He was no longer seen as someone that should be invited into the sphere of influence of the firm. He had devolved into a journeyman lawyer, and younger professionals began to wonder when he would retire and leave a space for them. Younger lawyers began to talk behind his back and refer to him in negative terms. At some level he believed that he had lost the race. This was the reward for being so committed to the law firm for all these years. He was rewarded not with a gold watch but with a gnawing in his stomach that he had not made it in life. He hadn't reached the goal like he thought he would.

Whether this lawyer's perception was accurate is irrelevant to this discussion. In his mind, he felt like a stranger in a strange land because he had not received appointment as the new department head. Despite his high level of competence and partnership status, he experienced that sense of figurative banishment and all the anxiety that comes with it.

Boundary of Inclusion

This third dimension is less tangible than the other two but no less important. It revolves around a perception of being aligned with and involved in the company's essence. It causes professionals to ask questions like: *Do I feel like I'm connected to the soul of the organization or family or team or group? Do I feel like I have voice in the direction and purpose of the organization? Do I believe that I play a role in this community, this organization even in some small but meaningful way?*

The behavior of professionals who perceive that they are no longer connected to the group or organization is very predictable. William, for instance, didn't receive an invitation to a particular committee meeting, and it was the third time the group had met that he hadn't been invited. After the first occurrence he just shook it off. The second noninvitation caused him to mention it to his spouse. This third time, though, William recognized that something was amiss and that he was no longer part of the group in this particular office that made the key decisions.

Rather than asking the group what was going on or discussing his feelings with a friend in the office or even speaking with the head of the office, William began to isolate himself. He ate lunch alone or with his assistant. He sat by himself for long stretches behind his closed office door. Perhaps even more troubling, he began spending a significant amount of time searching for evidence in the behaviors of others that reinforced his belief that he had become an outsider. William said, "I was convinced that I was no longer a player in the office. By that point I began to worry about my career and ignore my work. I was in an absolute tailspin."

Again, we see a professional wrapped up in anxiety because he perceived exclusion. In William's case, this perception is probably false, but it doesn't matter. William is convinced that it is reality, and his paranoid take on events impacts his work negatively. As his performance slides, his boss notices and perception becomes reality—no one wants to include William on key teams or in important meetings because his attention seems to have wandered. In response, William becomes more insular and disconnected. He is lucky if he is able to stay in the "do the wrong thing well" quadrant (figure 2-2). Even if he remains there, he lacks the sense of connection necessary to muster the confidence to take a chance and try something new that he won't be good at initially. So at best William is stuck in his quadrant, and at worse he's going to start doing the wrong thing poorly.

The Gravitational Pull

High-need-for-achievement professionals possess a *gravitational pull* to feel left out. If you're one of these people, you reflexively look for signs and signals that tell you you're being excluded or not wanted. The natural inclination is to withdraw and be alone and ruminate about how you have been excluded and abandoned by those who cared for you. It is a devastating feeling, one that is hard to understand and empathize with until you have experienced rejection or perceived that you have been voted off the island.

Be aware that you, rather than some external force, may be creating this gravitational pull. Earlier in the book I told you of the young associate, Steve, who lost faith in the boss (me) who delayed giving him feedback about his performance and waited until year-end to give him the news. Steve began to fabricate a reality that made his own story more palatable. He began to be convinced that his boss hadn't taken him on myriad trips and taken others on those trips because of the meeting snafu in Chicago months earlier. He now saw in every action of his boss evidence that his boss was biased and not supportive. No one could convince Steve of anything different. He was now sure that all his fabricated stories were a reality. He was sure that the story he created to fill in his cognitive gaps was gospel.

Mike Martin was one of the most gifted traders on Wall Street. Morgan Stanley, where I was working at the time, hired him away from a leading bank. Our top executives and other members of the firm celebrated with a trip to the firm watering hole. What could be better? They had lured a top producer from a top competitor. A month later, I received a call from Martin. He said, "Tom, I've come back home," referring to his return to the bank where he had previously been employed. I replied, "What do you mean you've come back home?" Hearing his response was like listening to a building implode and fall to the ground. He said, "I came back to my former firm because of the way I was treated. In a month only you came by my office to welcome me. Not one other managing director introduced himself or herself to me. I asked several times to have an assistant assigned to me. No one followed up. I've never been treated like this ever. I don't need this." I apologized. I said on behalf of the other partners we were sorry. He stopped me in midsentence and said to save my words and efforts to bring him back. He ended the conversation by stating that joining Morgan Stanley was the worst career decision he had ever made. Basically, we voted Martin off the island before he ever got on the island. We had excluded him and abandoned him before he arrived. Shame on me and shame on us as an institution.

And yet it wasn't intentional. It's not that organizations want to exclude people, especially their valued professionals. It's just that they fail to create ongoing, effective processes that make their people feel connected. In these environments, you can easily allow the gravitational pull to create a false perception. You conjure up scenarios in which people are ignoring you or deliberately excluding you. Rather than confronting these individuals or taking actions that force people to recognize your value and bring you into the inner circle, you allow your anxieties to get the better of you. You fume and fret and lose your sense of connection. At this point, it's difficult for you to change your ways or to take on tasks where you might look uncertain or take on a learner's role (rather than that of a teacher). Instead, you sink deeper into yourself, seeking refuge in the tasks that you know you can perform well. While this may moderate your anxieties to some extent—you feel better when you do something that you know you're good at—it doesn't endear you to others in the organization. Instead of stretching, growing, and achieving more ambitious goals, you're stuck in place.

To determine if you're caught in a gravitational pull of your own devising, see if you've ever been pulled downward by the following progressive forces:

1. An event takes place in your organization that makes you feel ignored, shunned, or excluded in some way.

2. You don't talk to anyone about what has happened; instead, you engage in a fierce internal dialogue that involves suspicions about your declining stature within the organization.

3. Rather than test your suspicions by talking with your boss or others, you allow them to fester and grow; they reach the point that they are no longer suspicions but convictions.

4. You start seeing evidence of your exclusion daily; you interpret everything from your boss's body language to a team member's offhand remark as irrefutable proof that you've been exiled.

5. Your anxiety level is high, and in response you decide your only recourse is to demonstrate your competence at the tasks you do best; you avoid or refuse any assignment that might make you look "bad."

6. You find that not only isn't the situation improving but that you're feeling more isolated than ever; you decide to look for another job or cleave to tasks that you feel comfortable with.

If this gravitational pull process feels familiar, recognize that you are perfectly capable of escaping it. Let's look at how you can do so.

Three Responses to Feelings of Isolation

Contrary to what you might think, especially if you're a driven professional convinced you're being ignored, you are capable of escaping the gravitational pull and restoring your feeling of belonging. The three keys, though, are what you do, when you do it and how you act. Let's start with the "when" first:

- Do something before your sense of isolation becomes entrenched.

If you ask people when they began to feel like they were excluded, the majority of them will mention some incident that occurred early in their tenure with a company, team, or group. Contrary to what you might think, the exclusionary response on the part of organizations isn't well-considered and based on performance over a period of time. Instead, it's largely rooted in personal response to an individual or event. It can also be illusory—a boss tosses off a remark and his driven, newly hired direct report misinterprets it. In either case, don't let the incident pass without dealing with it. If it's an inconsequential remark, you want to know that right away so that you don't become consumed by anxiety right from the start of your tenure. If someone does form a negative judgment about you, however, it's even more crucial to set the record right early; or, if you've made a mistake, to know what you need to do to correct it and feel included again.

I have seen many instances of organizations making quick, permanent judgments about new hires. One vice president admitted, "We pretty much decide in the first six to eight weeks whether or not we think the person is a star or future poor performer." When I pushed back a little to ask how they made the assessment and evaluated their new hires, the same vice president said, "It's largely by feel. It's also whether or not we enjoy hanging out with them." When I once again queried whether the judgment was based on the employees' competencies in doing the work, my friend paused and put his hands behind his head and smiled slowly. He then lamented, "I guess we should look more closely at their work. But we have been doing it this way for so long that I'm not sure we could change and make the process any different."

To correct negative first impressions, then, as well as for your own self-esteem, respond as soon as an incident causes your sense of isolation to surface:

- Step back and realize that you might be losing perspective.

- Communicate with the isolating party clearly, concisely, and honestly.

I understand that these are difficult conversations to initiate, whether you're a new hire or an old hand. High-need-for-achievement professionals dread having their worst fears confirmed: that they are indeed on the outs with their boss or the company and have fallen off the fast track. In most instances, however, these fears will be calmed or eliminated if you express yourself to your boss or other colleagues with candor and clarity. Don't go in and give a long speech about your fears or become defensive. Instead, quickly and simply state your concerns. The odds are that you'll be rewarded with reassuring statements about how you're a valued member of the company or receive helpful suggestions, either of which will moderate your feelings of isolation.

Sometimes you may feel isolated not because of what people say or do but because of what they *don't* do. Gordon, for instance, joined a *Fortune* 500 company after working for two smaller companies over a ten-year period. He had a sterling record—a top MBA program, compelling accomplishments at his two previous employers—and great things were expected of him. Yet for some reason, Gordon dropped off the radar screen at this company. It wasn't that he had done anything wrong—he just became lost in a large organization, in part because his groups were restructured shortly after he was hired and he was placed on a new team with a new boss. Though this new boss and team members were cordial, they rarely asked him to join them for lunch or, more significantly, gave him the type of challenging assignments he relished.

Gordon made two mistakes in response to this situation. First, he delayed having a conversation with his boss. Months passed before he finally mustered the courage to go into his boss's office and explain that he felt he'd been "shunted aside." And that was his second mistake. His anxiety had been building over a period of months, and so when he talked to his boss, he spent the first twenty minutes of their conversation listing all his grievances. Gordon's boss was taken aback—he had no idea that Gordon felt that way—and after a while, he was peeved at Gordon and suggested that if he felt this way, perhaps this wasn't the right place for him. His boss later told his own boss that he regretted making that harsh suggestion but that Gordon had aggravated him to the point that he found it difficult to be calm and civil.

Even though it's emotionally healthy and intellectually honest to communicate your concerns, take a moment and assess your motivations by doing the following:

- Ask yourself whether or not you may be overreacting.

- Ask yourself whether or not you have a pattern of taking perceived or real feedback too personally.

- Think about whether your organization and especially your
  CEO practices inclusion.

This last recommendation is not as difficult a determination to
make as it might appear. In the majority of cases, companies follow the
lead of their CEOs in this matter. If the top executive models behaviors that make people feel empowered and connected to the corporate
community, then this is a good place for high-need-for-achievement
professionals to be. When CEOs make it a point to solicit a diverse
group of opinions, when they reward others who work hard at growing their people (and not just delivering results), when they initiate
programs designed to help people at all levels learn and grow, then it's
likely the organization is inclusionary. Let me give you three examples
of inclusionary CEOs so you know what type of top bosses to look for.

John Mackey is the type of CEO who makes an extraordinary effort
to include rather than exclude. The chairman of Whole Foods knows
how to hire new employees and socialize them into the organization.
Mackey obsesses about inclusion and community. When someone is
hired in the cheese section of a Whole Foods store, all the cheese-
mongers interview the candidate and get a say in who gets hired and
who doesn't. It has to be a unanimous vote. The same holds true for
all the departments within a particular store. Why does everyone get
a say about who gets hired? Because Mackey wants to make sure that
everyone in the department is committed to the success of that new
person. Rather than waiting for the person to fail so that you can say,
"I told you so," you commit early on to helping that person succeed by
making him feel supported.

While Southwest Airlines receives many plaudits for its business
model, it should also receive credit for its policy of employee inclusion.
Colleen Barrett, Southwest's former president, explained, "We put
individuals on probation for a year before officially hiring them so that

it gives both parties the opportunity to see if there is a good fit. This time period sets the context that helps the individual manage expectations while giving the organization more time to see if they believe the person is a fit." Turnover rate continues to be infinitesimal compared to other airlines, customer service scores are consistently tops in the industry, and so many people want to work there that it's harder to get hired at Southwest than it is to get accepted at the Harvard Business School.

Finally, Tony Hsieh, chairman and CEO of Zappos (which was recently bought by Amazon), was obsessed about how to create an inclusive, committed team. Over time he realized that the socialization period of bringing on new hires was one of the keys to this endeavor, and he focused on creating a process in which people felt important and connected to Zappos. After three weeks of training, each recruit is offered $2,000 to leave the company and is given until the end of the day to decide. Virtually no one leaves. New hires feel included and aligned with the organization; they leave the training period committed to Zappos' purpose and processes.

Obviously, you don't always have the opportunity to choose your CEOs or companies. Not every CEO will be obsessed with inclusion like the three just mentioned. What I'm suggesting, though, is that you can use a CEO's style as a litmus test for inclusion. If your CEO favors a tight inner circle and disdains everyone else, if few programs exist to make people feel valued and to help develop their knowledge and skills, and if the chief executive isolates himself from most of his people, then it may be time to consider other employment options.

Now let's move on to the third cause of anxiety and stress in high-need-for-achievement professionals: diminished feelings of personal significance.

CHAPTER FIVE

Significance

Does Anybody but Me Care About Me?

THIS THIRD CAUSE OF ANXIETY IS PERHAPS more subtle than the other two, but no less insidious. What constitutes insignificance within an organization? Is it the lack of consistent encouragement from a boss? Is it a more general sense of being an easily replaced part? Is it a belief that your contributions are relatively inconsequential?

The answer is all of the above, and more. High-need-for-achievement professionals want to believe that their efforts matter, that other people value their work. For some, this need for significance is at the high end of the continuum—they require constant reassurance that they're highly valued members of the organization. For others, this need is at the low end—they just want the occasional pat on the back.

For most, though, it's not enough to be a well-paid professional in a prestigious organization. In and of themselves, these factors don't confer significance. Even if they are well-paid members of a top organization, professionals can rationalize their salaries and perks and believe they are simply benefiting from a kind boss who can't bear to tell them they don't matter or that they've pulled the wool over management's eyes.

To help you better understand how a lack of significance produces paralyzing anxiety; let me start with a story of a hard-charging executive stopped in her tracks by feelings of irrelevance.

A Loss of Personal Meaning and Professional Impact

Cara worked for a Big Three automaker in Michigan. Unlike many of her managerial colleagues, Cara grew up in a blue-collar environment—her father had worked on a Detroit assembly line—and attended a state school. Yet Cara had a passion for cars and a head for business, and she received dual degrees in engineering and business. When she was hired by her favorite automobile company right after graduation in the late '90s, she was ecstatic. Though Cara's company had had its ups and downs, it was in an up cycle at the time, and the future looked promising.

Though her entry-level position wasn't glamorous, she quickly impressed her boss with her knowledge and enthusiasm. Within a year, Cara was promoted to a position of greater responsibility, and soon she was being rotated through a series of functional assignments—marketing, engineering, finance, and two overseas postings—and being groomed for a leadership role. In her various jobs, Cara proved herself especially adept at matching new car design features with emerging consumer market trends. Cara regularly received superior performance reviews and sizable bonuses and base salary increases.

Everything was going great for the first ten years of her career. Then the recession hit, the auto industry suffered greatly, and Cara's company went into survival mode. Though many of her colleagues were fired, Cara made it through two downsizings. Her boss and mentor, however, did not, and Cara ended up being transferred to a division responsible for a line of cars that was gradually being phased out. Even worse, she was removed from the design and strategy assignments that were her strong suit and given largely financial responsibilities. On top of that, her new boss was essentially retired in place, and though he was perfectly nice toward Cara, he communicated little appreciation of her talents and provided scant feedback when she completed tasks. Her boss had essentially hit the pause button.

After a few months in this group, Cara felt as though she was in the wrong place for the first time in her working life. Though she had previously experienced a few bumps in her career path, she had moved past them with her combination of energy and knowledge. Now, though, Cara felt helpless. More troubling, she found herself going about her tasks with one eye on the clock. She told a friend that she could do her current assignments in her sleep. Cara desperately wanted to talk to someone about her situation, but she didn't know where to turn—the two top executives who had helped her in the past were gone—and she didn't want to appear as if she was ungrateful to still have a job when so many of her peers had lost theirs.

So Cara continued to competently perform a job she disliked, but she took no risks—she didn't volunteer for assignments, sign up for training programs, or request a transfer. She needed the job—she and her husband couldn't make their mortgage if one of them was out of work. But doing the wrong thing competently didn't help Cara professionally or personally. She lost her drive and desire to learn during this time. Even though she recognized she was a skilled, knowledgeable professional, she didn't feel like one. It was as if, at age thirty-five, she was on the verge of extinction. On her darkest days, she believed that she would never make a significant contribution to the company again.

And so she remained locked in place, unable and unwilling to change or grow.

Cara, like many high-need-for-achievement professionals, wanted to feel that her work mattered, that she was making a difference to her group and to her organization. For the first ten years of her career, she had found that significance, and thrived personally and professionally. When it diminished and then disappeared, Cara froze. She essentially went into a holding pattern in which she performed competently but avoided any type of change. Without feeling like her work mattered, she became extremely anxious when it came to trying something new. Change was exactly what Cara needed, but change is what she avoided.

Given all the talk in the business world about creating work "communities" and providing employees with meaningful, fulfilling jobs, you would think savvy leaders would recognize the need to help people like Cara find significance in their work. No doubt, most leaders may want to help their people feel significant. Unfortunately, they often are unable to do so. Let's look at what goes on in a typical organization and why it may fail to respond to your need to feel that you're doing significant work.

Indifference Toward Your Need to Make a Difference

To understand the importance of significance in your work life, recall a time when you were out of work—even a self-imposed or brief sabbatical. It doesn't have to be a despairing time after you were fired from a job. You may have been able to spend more time with your family, pursue a hobby, or take that long-dreamed-about trip to some foreign land. Nonetheless, the odds are that if you're a high-need-for-achievement professional, you found yourself wondering if you mattered anymore. At first this thought may have emerged as a glimmer in the back of your mind, but the longer you weren't working, the bigger it grew.

One friend, a CEO, left an organization and took his time landing another leadership position. About that interim period, he said, "What I missed the most was the affirmation. It was knowing that I was making a difference in the lives of others. It was the feeling that I was good at what I did, others valued what I did, and—arrogantly speaking— that if I left, the organization might even take a step backwards. I know this last comment is a bit delusional but I'm willing to live with that illusion."

Do you experience similar feelings of insignificance? Do you experience them even when you are working?

What is surprising is how oblivious many managers are to their people's sense of significance. Look at the following list and consider the last time your boss or some other influential member of your organization did the following:

- Asked you how you were doing

- Told you that you were doing a good job

- Asked you if he/she could help in any way

- Suggested that the company or your group wouldn't be where it is without your efforts

- Demonstrated to you the positive impact your work had on a larger organizational goal

- Requested your participation on a team or project deemed crucial to the company

- Made you feel like a task you recently completed was not only appreciated but essential for the forward progress of your group

- Said how much he or she and the larger group were depending on you

It's likely that you can't place a check next to any item on the list, at least when you think about your work experiences from the last few months. Many companies are experiencing *results myopia*—they are locked into productivity and profit measures. Consequently, many organizations lack the consciousness to address issues of significance and meaning among their professionals.

Within any organization, there exist high-need-for-achievement professionals who are in need of affirmation: older members of the organization who feel their years relegate them to over-the-hill status; midlevel people who are undergoing midcareer self-evaluations, second-guessing their career choices, and wondering if they should be doing something more significant; and younger professionals who are struggling to find their place in the organizational world. No matter which group you belong to, you want to feel like your work matters. Unfortunately, your bosses may not realize the importance of communicating this sentiment and tailoring it to you. To understand why this sentiment isn't being communicated, let's focus on a specific group: ambitious professionals who are members of the Millennial generation.

Some veteran leaders believe this generation has an attitude problem. Millennials want everything now. They feel entitled. They have been raised on the computer and they expect instantaneous response and information from everything and everyone. Because of their attitude, young people possess unrealistic expectations of life in organizations, or so the argument goes.

While I'm sure plenty of young employees fit that description, I can find many others who don't. I suspect that the majority of young people act the way they do in work situations because their *bosses* have attitude problems. Specifically, they don't make a consistent effort to acknowledge the contributions these young employees make. Perhaps, just perhaps, managers and mentors are not managing or mentoring. Perhaps managers and mentors feel so burdened by all their responsibilities and assignments that the one thing that slides is taking the time to connect with those who are new to the organization, or to those who have moved laterally at midcareer.

A partner in a prestigious London law firm complained, "Why should I spend time with our young associates? At the end of the day they are going to leave anyway. They have less commitment to us. The data show that very few of them will be at the firm in three to five years. So why should I waste my time and put in hours with these kids knowing that I'm wasting my time?"

The following exercise is a highly effective litmus test for feelings of significance, and it's one that younger employees tend to have problems with:

> *Write the name of the best leader, teacher, or coach you've ever had. Write the name of the individual who made a difference in your life, who seemed to care more about you and your career than you cared about yourself.*

You'll find that if you're over age forty, you are able to name at least one person, and often two or more. Typically, one of these individuals is a boss you had. If you're younger than forty, however, you may come up with one name, but it's rarely someone with whom you've worked; you name an athletic coach or a high school teacher. Having administered this exercise to executives of many types and ages in recent years, I can tell you that this is almost always how the answers skew.

We have a vicious cycle operating in many organizations. Senior leaders blame the young MBAs for being naive and entitled, and assume that the younger generation arrives at the company with "negative" attitudes intact. These younger employees, however, form this attitude only because they are in desperate need of someone who cares about them, who communicates that they matter, who lets them know they make a difference. They don't need positive feedback when it isn't deserved. What they need are managers and leaders who are aware that they want to feel significant and who make the effort to communicate this fact in small as well as big ways.

I'm not absolving you of responsibility for finding your own significance in a career or a job. No matter whether you're a young, middle-aged, or older professional, if you're driven to achieve, you also need to be driven to find your place in a work setting. You can't depend on an organization to make a concerted and consistent effort to imbue your work with meaning.

Recognize that the challenges of finding significance are in part based on your age, in part on your social motives and values, in part on your mental makeup (e.g., are you in the midst of divorce or other life crisis?), in part on your work situation (e.g., the company may be going through a massive downsizing or culture change), and in part on management's approach to this issue. While you can't control some of these factors, you can control your response to them.

You need to define and redefine what type of work you want to do, what type of organization and culture you want to be part of, and what goals you want to strive for. And you need to do this regularly, since what's significant now might not be as significant a year from now. For some of you, working for the leading organization in your field may be of prime significance. For others, working in a smaller, closer-knit culture is what matters.

Finally, if you want to increase the odds that your organization will help you find significance in your work, look for the modern equivalent of the apprenticeship model. Professional services firms used to be structured as stratified apprenticeships, and within this system, learning, mentoring, growth, and accountability were integral components. Though many firms have moved away from this model, a number of companies maintain it in spirit if not in formal structure.

Seek work in companies where young people, those new to an organization, and even some veteran employees starting out on new jobs and tasks essentially serve as apprentices to "master craftsmen." This entails a lot of learning on the job—following senior people around, asking questions, being questioned, trying, failing, and then succeeding. Apprentices naturally feel significant, since their master is responsible for them and their education—they receive continuous feedback, their learning and progress is monitored, and when they are ready, they are promoted into positions of responsibility. In this way, they achieve significance.

You want to find an organization where senior professionals enjoy mentoring rather than resent the time required and billable hours lost. You want to work for a company where your learning and growth is valued, where you are treated as a distinct individual rather than a replaceable part. Finding this type of company is more challenging today than years ago, but it's worth the effort, since finding it will go a long way in helping you find the significance you seek.

The Solid-Citizen Challenge

Not every high-need-for-achievement professional is seen as a fast-tracker or high-potential. Some are quietly ambitious, driven to achieve yet not driven to call attention to themselves. Others may have started out being tabbed as high-potentials but as they grew and as the company changed, they settled into a particular niche and were seen as terrific producers rather than budding superstars. Still others are simply overlooked—they are capable of achieving greatness yet for one reason or another, they are categorized as B players.

In fact, the number of high-potentials within any organization is relatively small, while the number of solid citizens is relatively large. So the odds are, you may find yourself in this second group at some point in your career, no matter how high-revving your internal drive is. If so, you probably will find yourself questioning your significance.

That's because the good, solid citizens of the organization go largely unnoticed. Few leaders at any level in an organization strategically think about the motivation, inclusion, and explicit career management of the solid performers. One leader of a *Fortune* 500 company said, "I thought to myself that it couldn't be true that so many workers in organizations are systematically ignored through no fault of their own (except for the fact that they may not be politically astute or they don't draw attention to themselves). But then the more I reflected on my own company, the more I realized that I spend all my time worrying about the high performers and assume that everything is OK with everyone else."

What all this suggests is that if you're a solid citizen, you shouldn't wait for others to make you feel significant. Instead, you need to make sure that you're doing the work that you find meaningful, you need to communicate what your contributions are to your boss and other influencers, and you need to speak out if you find yourself stuck in a rut that feels meaningless and unfulfilling.

Categorize Yourself:
Find Your Quadrant of Significance

Figure 5-1 depicts how most organizations classify their employees. Most organizations have their own unique grid that tries to balance the characteristics of performance and living values of the institution. The Y axis focuses on how a professional is measured on meeting the organizational performance criteria that fuel the business engine.

FIGURE 5-1

Quadrant of significance

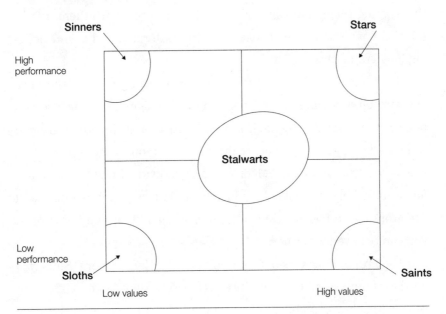

The X axis centers on how the professional fares on meeting the expectations along the dimension measuring the human engine. If you know your quadrant, you can predict how the organization will deal with you—the degree to which it will (or will not) provide mentoring, coaching, feedback, growth opportunities, and the like. With this knowledge, you can go into a situation with realistic expectations of your organization—expectations that can help you prevent the anxiety that comes when you feel (wrongly, in many instances) that the organization doesn't care about you and isn't concerned whether you're effective, challenged, and so on.

In the upper right corner are the top performers ("Stars") who can do it all (and know it). They are the employees who demand to be told that they are significant and special and unique. One manager complained, "For my top performers, I have to tell them on Monday how good they are but that's not enough. They will be in my office or on the phone again by Thursday wanting to know that you remember them, value them, and think the sun rises and sets with them. I can't tell you how much time is soaked up in reinforcing and acknowledging how grand they are."

So if this describes you, you may be receiving pats on the back and stretch assignments, but you may feel insignificant because you believe the positive feedback is perfunctory or insincere. You need to find a boss, mentor, or other influential person in the organization whom you trust implicitly. Meet with this individual regularly and ask for brutally honest feedback, guidance, and ideas. If you're doing well and working up to your capacity, this person will let you know—and you can believe him or her.

The group of professionals rated in the top left corner ("Sinners") hit their numbers and are very productive, but they can be difficult to work with; they can abuse other people but get away with it because they are highly productive. John Mack of Morgan Stanley related his perspective on a meeting held to determine who would be promoted: "If we promote professionals who hit their numbers and yet are bad managers then we have no values, it's all talk. It's easy to demand that professionals live the values when they are average performers. But you can't blink when making tough decisions about those [who] make their numbers on the backs of others."

If you're a great producer but aren't receiving the type of promotions and performance reviews that reflect this production, you may feel a deep sense of dissatisfaction with your overall performance. When you miss out on a promotion to a job you coveted, you may feel like you're not as good as you thought, that you have a fatal flaw in your makeup. In fact, you need to develop your people skills to be a complete professional and gain the satisfaction that comes with being whole. Coaching may help. So too may a greater awareness of your deficiencies in dealing with people. You're not going to change completely or overnight, but if you can moderate some of your worst tendencies, you'll achieve more than you have and feel that much better about yourself moving forward.

In the lower left corner of figure 1-5 are those individuals who are not connected with the organization cognitively, emotionally, or in their productivity. Organizations that are flush with money often let these underperformers be, but become tougher on them when money constricts. Employees and organizations are complicit in letting the situation reach this point. The company writes off these people as hiring mistakes, and the employees in turn have no reason to perform well since they are being shunned by the organization. Rather than confront them with honest conversations, their bosses make the environment so miserable for them that they eventually leave on their own. Some of these employees wait to be fired to get a better severance package.

If you're in this difficult quadrant, it's time to request assistance from your boss or a coach. You may well have been pushed toward insignificance without ever receiving coaching or having anyone set expectations for you and provide support so you can meet firm expectations. Ideally, you'll find a leader with power, authority, and influence who is willing to spend time with you and help you feel as if you matter. Without this type of intervention, you're going to remain mired in insignificance.

The group in the lower right quadrant ("Saints") are similar to those in the lower left, with one fundamental difference: they love the organization and work to build the culture. They bleed company colors. The problem is that the more they try and build culture, the more others view their efforts as an excuse for not producing acceptable financial outcomes. Again, organizational managers have difficulty confronting these professionals, in large part because they are

just great people and community focused. They care about the organization so much that it's hard to have difficult conversations with
them and set specific time frames and goals they must meet in order
to improve their performance.

If you're in this quadrant, you may feel a diminished sense of
significance because you know or sense that others don't view you
as productive. The odds are that deep down inside, you know you
aren't productive yet you want to be valued for being a good corporate citizen. It may be tough for your boss to hold your feet to
the fire and it may be tough for you if he does so, but it's the best
way for you to feel that you're making a real difference in the organization. As we'll see, accountability has a direct bearing on employees' feelings of significance in all quadrants, but especially in
this one.

Accountability: A Tough but Effective
Way to Confer Significance

Parenting provides us with a good analogy for this final point about
significance. Kids want to be held accountable by their parents, even
though they may not always act like it. They want their parents to
expect them to get good grades, to clean up their rooms, to be home
by the time they say they'll be home. Why? Because when you hold
someone accountable, you communicate that you care about them.
When you tell kids you expect them to get good grades, you're telling them that you know they have the intelligence and drive to do
well academically, and that you care about them enough that you want
them to reach their potential. As a result, when a child receives a good
grade in a class, he feels as if he's done something meaningful, not just
because of the good grade but because he has met the high standard
set for him by his parents.

The same principle holds true in work situations. If the boss holds us accountable for ambitious work goals, he communicates that he values what we do and our ability to do it, that the group needs us to achieve those objectives. The weight of these high expectations can produce some stress, but it can also produce a sense of significance—a more than reasonable trade-off. Think about when your boss or a customer demanded that you stretch to achieve a tough objective. You know there was a hard-and-fast number you had to make, a deadline you had to adhere to, a difficult skill you had to master. But when you did so successfully, you felt as if you had accomplished something that mattered.

So demand accountability from clients and customers, bosses and colleagues. Make sure you communicate the specific objectives on which you want them to measure your performance. Understand, it's not going to be easy for you or them. You don't want to be judged, since you're concerned that you'll come up short. They don't want to judge you, because they're concerned they may have to have a difficult conversation with you. Yet this is a win-win situation that makes accountability worth it.

As much as, if not more than, inclusion and purpose, significance keeps our anxiety at bay. When we believe we're making a difference or doing work that is fulfilling, we're not working scared. We don't fret over every offhand comment our boss makes or become paranoid and believe that we have fallen from favor and will never regain it. Instead, when we believe in what we're doing, we believe in ourselves. This gives us the courage to take on new projects and master new skills; we no longer are as anxious about doing the right thing poorly. We can take a chance without fearing our vulnerability. As high-need-for-achievement professionals, we yearn for significance more than most. It reassures us and satisfies our need to have an impact through our work.

Think of insignificance as well as isolation and lack of purpose as obstacles on the road to leading more productive, fulfilling lives. When we run into these obstacles, instead of finding a way around them we skid off the road into traps that make our problems worse. In the following chapters I'll explain what these traps are and how they paralyze us and keep us from changing.

PART III

THE FOUR TRAPS THAT KEEP YOU FROM CHANGE

CHAPTER SIX

Busyness

The First of the Higher Powers

W HEN HIGH-NEED-FOR-ACHIEVEMENT professionals become anxious—when they feel isolated, lacking in purpose, and insignificant—they often find it difficult to rise above these feelings and see another view. Instead of confronting their anxiety and making the behavioral and work changes that will further their growth, these individuals plunge deeper into their anxieties. Why don't these bright, ambitious professionals see what is happening to them? Why are they unable to muster the courage to make themselves vulnerable to fresh challenges and new experiences, to change in ways that will allow them to flourish?

Because they're trapped. Here and in chapters 7, 8, and 9, I'll examine the four traps that keep people stuck, provide them with little satisfaction, and limit their productivity. These traps guide how people behave, how they see the world, how they spend their time avoiding being honest with themselves when they become anxious.

The traps are not presented in any particular order; the first is just as insidious as the fourth. Though each has a distinctive way in which it ensnares unsuspecting high-need-for-achievement types, they all keep professionals from addressing their purpose, their fear of isolation and disconnection, and their need to feel significant.

Are you trapped? This question isn't always easy to answer, since these traps operate in ways that are subtle and nuanced. On the surface, you may appear to be productively engaged in your work and doing well; it takes a trained eye to see the dysfunction beneath the surface.

If you're not progressing in your development toward a goal or purpose that matters, you're likely caught in a trap. The only sign of life is growth. Even with this litmus test, you may refuse to accept or admit that you're trapped. Denial is a danger for many driven professionals whose egos prevent them from facing the facts of their situations. Instead, they settle into their anxiety-lined traps, working competently if not exceptionally, feeling okay about their work but not great. It's a limbo of sorts, and while it might not feel horrible, it has a horrible result—people aren't working up to their capacities or willing to stretch themselves.

Let's first turn to a trap that many of you are familiar with: *busyness*.

Busy Running in Place

If you've ever raced from one meeting to the next and occupied hours responding to emails, you may have fallen into the busyness trap. Yes, many high-need-for-achievement professionals have a lot to do, and it's possible to be busy with challenging, meaningful work. But when you're busy for busyness's sake—when you take on mundane, repetitive tasks just to make sure you look and feel like you're accomplishing something—then it's possible that your anxiety has driven you into this trap.

Think about how you appear to others when they first enter your office, watch you walk through the hallways, or engage in a conversation with you. In these unguarded moments, do they observe any of the following traits:

- Your face is tight, and a sense of urgency is conveyed by your every move.

- During conversations, you make a show of listening but seem to be counting the seconds until you can move on to the next thing.

- You walk fast, talk fast, and create the impression you are purposeful and relevant.

- You never appear to be lost in thought; you're always talking or reading or checking your computer or handheld screen.

If you're honest with yourself, how much of your frenetic pace and harried attitude is for show? Deep down, do you believe that if you run fast enough and distract others enough, somehow your worries will disappear? Let me introduce you to a high-need-for-achievement professional who is caught in the busyness trap.

Sal, a vice president of a large advertising agency, is criticized behind his back for not thinking strategically; people also complain that his meetings go nowhere and that he seems to jump from meeting to meeting but no decisions are ever made or process completed. One team member told me over drinks, "Sal is so frightened of being irrelevant and being found out that he doesn't know what he's talking about when he comes into a meeting. There is no discussion. There is no decision making. We are simply a group of individuals who come together and put up with a charade. If these meetings are only informational, then I shouldn't have to get on a plane and fly across the country to be told what I could have learned on e-mail." Sal mentions at least once in every conversation how many e-mails and voice mails wanted his attention; he uses his schedule to create the illusion that he is important. In other words, Sal fills his agenda with activities, but too often they are activities for activities' sake. By booking himself solid, by calling for meetings and commanding people to attend them, by e-mailing and cell-phone calling constantly, he convinces himself that he is achieving. In fact, he is unable to engage in the difficult conversations and make the tough decisions that are necessary for true achievement.

A close friend related the following story:

When I was launching my career years ago, I was guilty of a related busyness sin. I would come home from work exhausted, having given everything to the school, its students, other faculty—and of course having been busy with my own projects. My wife was just as tired, having managed three young girls, helped them with their homework, worked in her counseling practice, and managed the farmer who worked our farm, who always needed attention. I would jump in as enthusiastically as I could. I'm sure from my wife's perspective it seemed more perfunctory than enthusiastic.

When it came time to read a book to the kids, the first thing I did was encourage them to choose a book with a big font and few words or with many pictures so I could get through the book faster. If that strategy didn't work, I would try and read fast. But that irritated them. When the girls were really young, I would try skipping pages; I would actually try and distract the girls and quickly skip pages to get to the end faster. I wanted to get the kids in bed as fast as I could so that I could get back to my e-mails and voice mails and focus on those things that were "important" for me. What was really important, of course, was maintaining my self-perception as a busy guy, as someone who must be doing things right because he didn't even have the time to complete a story he was reading to his children.

I don't want to give the impression that it's just young professionals on the rise who fall into the busyness trap. If you've ever worked for an entrepreneurial start-up that became successful, you've probably witnessed the phenomenon of the *lame duck founder*. Founders are pivotal to these start-ups, using their vision and energy to launch the enterprise. Yet after the company becomes established, they often struggle to find their place. Typically, these founders feel left out as a management team is put in place. Founders make up titles for themselves that convey a sense of importance and responsibility, but in fact are just window dressing. The more obsolete they become, the harder they try to look busy. They may write white papers pontificating on a current issue, or create and head internal task forces with important-sounding goals. They may dominate meetings and schedule numerous business trips, but it's all to no avail. Their fellow workers are not stupid. They have observed their company's founders becoming more and more conscious that their work adds little value. While they remain loyal to the organization and want to build the culture, they essentially stay locked in place, doing the same things they did when they founded the company, experiencing little personal and professional growth, and contributing very little to the company. While they may believe their busy schedules and prestigious new titles create the image of a dynamic leader, others see that they are trying too hard to be busy.

After one start-up grew to five hundred people, there was little for one of the cofounders to do. Eventually, after a number of title and office changes, he settled on *chief culture officer*. No sooner had the e-mail gone out than professionals in different offices began calling one another and laughing, mocking the absurd moniker. One subordinate called him the "COO of Nothing." This may seem like a harmless thing, but it's harmful on two levels. First, this chief culture officer is fooling himself into thinking that he's doing something meaningful. His self-important position may keep him busy creating new slogans and implementing new policies related to his company's culture, but it prevents him from doing the sort of tough self-examination and reflection that might extricate him from his trap. Instead, he can fool himself into believing that he's taken on a vital new role when he's basically just taking up office space.

Second, giving oneself such a title may seem merely humorous during good times, but during tough economic periods it harms morale. Then, people respond not with mocking laughter but with anger and cynicism. The tone of the remarks made behind the chief culture officer's back becomes hostile, resentful, and bitter, and cynicism begins to eat away at the fabric of the institution.

We also use busyness to cover up our need for inclusion, purpose, and significance when we hit a rough patch in our careers—we encounter a bad boss or experience a bad fit in an organization. We first try to look and feel busy in order to prove to a boss that, despite his misgivings and criticism, we are dedicated and productive. We make a great show of working late or coming in early to convince people that, despite not fitting an organization's needs, we take our job seriously. These busy behaviors, however, are a charade. In fact, they're done not just to prove to others that we're industrious but also to prove it to ourselves.

We live in fear that we will be found out, that others will learn that we are adding basically nothing to the enterprise. We fear admitting this truth to ourselves, and being found out would bring shame and humiliation. Those emotions are anathema to high-need-for-achievement professionals who thrive on a lofty self-image. Therefore, we do all we can to avoid having nowhere to go and nothing significant to do. Being busy helps us avoid the embarrassment of not working up to our potential. More important, we may not want to admit that we don't know what to do with ourselves, either personally or professionally.

Feeding the Illusion

I frequently talk to MBA students about their careers and aspirations for life. Some of these students worked on Wall Street, and when we talk, a number of them admit that the key to success was creating the illusion of hard work. One said that he and the other associates would leave their suit coats on their chairs at the end of the work day to make it seem that they hadn't left for the night, that they were somewhere in the building doing work when in fact they had gone home. "We have these little tricks of the trade to create the impression that we are absolutely committed to the organization even when we don't have any work," he told me. It's part of managing expectations and our images."

These individuals have been in organizations long enough to know that racing behavior is what gets them ahead. Those chosen for top positions and rewarded with raises and titles tend to be the ones who appear to be running the fastest—working long hours, willing to travel constantly, able to finish labor-intensive projects by deadline. The problem is that the reward for winning this race is more work, which means people need to work harder at managing the illusion that they are busy. As one colleague who worked for a top-tier law firm suggested when he became partner: "The reward for winning the pie-eating contest is more pie."

Busyness has become a reflex for many high-need-for-achievement professionals, a reflex that is encouraged by our high-tech world. I saw a particular manifestation of this reflex when running seminars and programs for managers. One company spent countless dollars to fly its country managers from around the world in order to learn about the process of organizational change during a leadership development program. As part of this program, the organization wanted its managers to get to know one another, teach each other, and create a global network within the organization. When I finished the first session and paused for a thirty-minute break, the seventy participating managers barely spoke during that time. Instead, they immediately pulled out their PDAs and began reading their e-mails and text messages and sending their own. At some point during the half-hour they would quickly take a bathroom break or grab a second cup of coffee, then would go right back to their e-mails without making eye contact with anyone. These were important managers. They had a great deal of responsibility. They needed to stay connected. But it seemed as though they had missed one of the key reasons for getting together.

You could watch these managers over the days, walking around the conference center completely immersed in their hand-held devices. Was their electronic messaging so critical that they couldn't bother to communicate with their fellow managers? My suspicion is that while these managers were out of the office, they became anxious about work. They started worrying about what was going on in their absence. They found false reassurance with their frantic e-mailing and messaging; it helped them allay their anxieties and feel connected with work. In reality, of course, it was one way to avoid open and honest conversations with fellow managers—conversations that might have challenged them and called some of their beliefs into question.

Over lunch at a board meeting a few months back, I realized that an individual's attitude toward vacations was a good measuring stick for their busyness behaviors. One of the board members, Miriam, cap-tured the dynamics involved in the high-need-for-achievement per-sonality's busyness impulse: "When I'm busy I don't feel guilty. When I slow down I feel terrible about myself. I feel worthless." She then laughed and continued,

> When I'm the busiest is when I feel the best about taking a vacation, because for some reason I feel like I earned it. [But] it's the worst time to take time off. And I typically don't enjoy it that much because I'm worried about work back home. Last winter, when work was very slow, it would have been the per-fect time to take time off. I could have taken a month off and no one would have cared. In fact, my boss encouraged it. Of course, I made myself think there was important work to be done in order to justify myself. But I was just filling time. I felt too guilty to take time off under those circumstances.

She shook her head again with embarrassment as she realized how neurotic she sounded. But I observed numerous heads nodding around the table. I also knew that she was describing me.

In fact, Miriam unknowingly created a couple of excellent mea-sures for whether people are caught in the busyness trap:

- If the only time you really want to take a vacation is when work projects are overwhelming and you feel snowed under with tasks

- If you're most resistant to taking a vacation when work is slow, your boss is happy to have you take some time off, and no one will miss you while you're gone

Think about these two measures in terms of your own behaviors when you took time off. Was it at an incredibly hectic, stressful time for you? Was it a period when you really couldn't afford to be away from the office? Conversely, how many times did you fail to take vacations during your company's slowest periods last year? Vacations are frightening for many high-need-for-achievement professionals, since they are the antithesis of being busy. If you find your feelings about vacations are odd—if you want to take vacations at the worst possible time and resist taking vacations at the best possible time—then it's likely you're ensnared by the busyness trap.

The Power of the Insurance Salesman

I've conditioned everyone around me to know that I'm busy and important in my own mind. Like most high-need-for-achievement professionals, I didn't consciously communicate to others that my time was precious and that I was on call 'round-the-clock, but I sent this message loudly and clearly, not only to my work colleagues but to my family. As the hectic dinner hour approached in our home one day, I was standing near the bottom of the stairs. One of my daughters approached me and began to cry. A test for which she had studied for hours had questions that were different than she had expected. She was angry at the teacher and embarrassed because she had not listened to the teacher during the review. She was jealous of her friend who had done superbly. I tried to explain that I had done poorly on a number of tests, and I knew she would recover and do well in the class. As she poured out her troubles, the phone rang. I left my daughter and answered the phone, thinking it might be a work-related call. The person on the other end was cold-calling people in order to sell insurance that was the "best deal" ever for anyone who had the sense to buy it. As I told the salesman I wasn't interested, I watched out of the corner of my eye and saw my daughter walk up the stairs. I quickly hung up and followed her. The first thing Sara said was, "So the phone call was more important than talking with me?" She turned and walked to her room.

The moral of this story isn't just that you need to get your priorities straight. Certainly it is one lesson—falling into the trap of busyness can have a negative impact on your personal life and those you care about most—but there is another one: recognize that you cling to your busyness reflex irrationally. Organizations are filled with people who respond like Pavlov's dog to a "you've got mail" signal, an instant message beep, a cell-phone ring. They may rationalize this response, telling themselves it could be the boss with an emergency or a team member who needs their wisdom. But responding in this manner should tell people that who they are both at work and at home is not the individual they could be. Just as I used the phone to escape an emotional and important conversation with my daughter, people at work use their busyness as an excuse to avoid having meaningful conversations with colleagues. They use busyness to avoid engaging in the type of reflection that can help them learn something about their weaknesses as a manager, to avoid taking on an assignment or making a decision that might reveal they aren't as knowledgeable or in control as they'd like people to think.

Home as Pit Stop

I've been enamored with car racing since the days that Graham Moss and Phil Hill raced Formula One cars. This interest naturally segued into stock car racing. I loved watching David Pearson, Cale Yarborough, Fireball Roberts, Richard Petty, and others compete in this dangerous sport. But what really interested me were the pit stops—the lightning-quick time-outs that each car would make for fuel, new tires, or any assistance that was required. In fact, there are now pit crew competitions: forty pit crews, made of up to eight members, who race against each other to show their talents and abilities to beat the rest in transforming a car so that it's ready to get back on the track. During a race under pressure, crews can change five lug nuts on one tire in less than a second. They can change all four tires and refuel the car in ten seconds. It is the ultimate example of teams working with tremendous efficiency and speed.

One Saturday after a long week, I was channel surfing and saw that a race was taking place. It was midway through the race and very exciting. The eventual winner was able to leverage his pit crew to gain valuable seconds and to get out of the pit area faster than his key opponent. As I was watching the race, it dawned on me that my home was often about as hectic and busy as a pit stop. Every member of the family was going in a different direction. The conversation around the dinner table was basically about logistics—who would pick up whom when, how we would coordinate myriad activities.

We were living in Westchester County, north of New York City, in a nice house. But we really didn't need the house. We just needed a room with a big basket that would catch keys, notebooks, and various items that we used to get through the day. The difference between our family and the pit crew is that the crew had practiced and perfected the process of dealing with pressure. We were more like a bunch of undisciplined mechanics frantically trying to do something for which we had no process to do well. What I also realized was that I was teaching my daughters the importance of being busy and focused on an individual agenda. I was teaching them that busyness was more important than listening and caring for those who are supposed to mean the most to you. I realized that when I walked across the room and left my crying daughter to herself, I was reinforcing that busyness was happiness.

My children realized early on, they tell me now, that dad lived with the assumption that any break in the race put him behind. And being busy was proof that dad was in the race and pushing for the lead. Fortunately, they had enough additional experiences to recognize this was an illusion. The best pit crews are busy with a process and a purpose beyond winning the race; the individual members take pride in their work and are always trying to improve by testing new tools and techniques. The great pit crews don't just look busy for busyness's sake. Instead, they want to perform to the best of their abilities.

Raising Busyness Consciousness

The trap of busyness is that it's so much a part of us that we simply don't get what's really going on. We expect to be busy; we don't know what to do when we're not. In fact, the trap of busyness causes us to move with such mindless speed that we're like the proverbial chicken running around with his head cut off. We plunge into our e-mails and meetings with a manic energy that forbids reflection, deeply honest conversations, and breaks from the routine.

And at some level we know that this trap is designed to shield us from our anxieties. Many times, though, our awareness is fleeting. We need to raise that awareness. To that end, use the following questions to raise busyness consciousness:

- Do you believe your work allows you to move toward a specific and important goal—greater responsibility, learning a key new skill, achieving a capstone position?

- Do you find yourself attempting to create the appearance that you're busier than you really are? Do you start typing furiously on your computer when your boss walks in your office? Do you make it a point to emphasize how much travel you've undertaken on the company's behalf and the sacrifices you've made? Do you usually mention to your colleagues how late you've worked or how you spent the weekend working on a project, or how many e-mails you have to respond to?

- Are you addicted to your PDA or other forms of electronic communication? Are you constantly checking for messages? Are you unable to sustain conversations with work colleagues or family or friends without regularly checking for messages?

- When things slow down at work, do you feel guilty? Do you find it impossible to take a vacation when things are slow? Do you attempt to fill your free work time with meaningless and boring tasks?

- If you're busy, what percentage of that work is meaningful and challenging? What percentage of that work could be delegated to a subordinate without any drop-off in effectiveness? What percentage could be ignored completely without negative consequence?

- Have your family or friends ever commented on your need to feel important? Do they make fun of your inability to stop talking about work-related matters or enjoy personal time without communicating via cell phone or e-mail?

Once you recognize your impulse to cling to minor and relatively meaningless tasks—or any tasks, for that matter—you are in a better position to let go of some of them. And how do you let go? Admittedly, it's tough to break the habit of checking texts and e-mails regularly and managing our other busy behaviors. While everyone has to find his best way of getting these behaviors under control, here are some tactics that you might find useful:

- Impose a one-hour per day electronic blackout period; force yourself to designate this period during the workday to engage in reading, writing, or reflection, and avoid electronic busywork.

- Borrow a page from academics and establish office hours; designate times when your office is open for people to come in and talk with you about anything besides specific job tasks; use this time to have relaxed dialogues rather than objective-driven exchanges.

- Reduce your worst busyness behavior in small increments; if you average four hours a day on the phone, try to reduce that time by fifteen minutes; if you average one hundred thousand air miles annually, try to cut back to eighty thousand miles.

You don't have to go from manically busy to a state of Buddhalike contemplation, nor should you. As a driven, ambitious professional, you're not going to be happy or productive if you just sit around contemplating higher-level business concepts. The goal here is to escape the busyness trap, and you can do so if you just learn to manage the behaviors that make you frantic rather than eliminate them. This will free you to make more significant changes in how you work, providing you with the time and perspective to try new ideas and approaches.

Now let's turn our attention to the second trap: *comparing*.

CHAPTER SEVEN

Comparing

How to Break Your Heart Every Time

IN THE WORLD OF SOCIAL SCIENCES, the technical term for comparing ourselves with others is *social relativity*. It is the process of using external measures to determine how we think we are doing, of defining our successes by external criteria. This process begins early in life, and it is instilled in us by many factors. In fact, the process is so baked into everything we experience that it often feels like we have no control over the emotions that cause us to compare ourselves to others. It becomes a reflex rather than a calculated action. In certain cultures, the process of comparing impacts behavior all the time and in every way.

Within the Morgan Stanley culture, managing directors compared constantly and in many work dimensions. For instance, two manag-

ing directors were at roughly the same level of experience and responsibility, yet one made $25,000 more than the other—a fact that
became apparent to the lesser-paid of the two and made him furious.
This created a great deal of tension between the two, since neither of
them could see the larger picture and grasp that the logic behind the
pay disparity. Because they had fallen into the comparing trap, I had
a management problem that lasted too long. More to the point, they
had a problem because they became focused on who had what—salary,
size of office, job title—rather than on learning, growth, development,
and accomplishment. They devoted most of their energy to comparison battles instead of hoisting themselves out of their routines and
exploring ways of communicating.

Comparing is a trap that permeates our lives, especially if we're
high-need-for-achievement professionals. When we are questioning
our purpose in life and our identity, comparing goes into overdrive.
When we question our significance at work or in a broader way, we
are trying to manipulate our environment to get the feedback we
crave in order to experience some sense of affirmation. When we are
feeling alone and isolated, we suddenly see the world in the context
of how others are grouped or behaving in groups. Or our comparing takes an even more negative form: we look for reasons why we
should be alone and don't deserve to be attached to other communities or groups. No matter how successful we are and how many goals
we achieve, this trap causes us to recalibrate our accomplishments
and reset the bar for how we define success. What we've done in the
past doesn't matter; *real* success or achievement requires something
more—a title we've never held, a task we've never done, a company
we've never worked for. The process of comparing requires us to keep
making our target more difficult to hit. And if we manage to hit this difficult target, we simply create an even more difficult one at which we
can aim.

No matter how much we achieve, we are never satisfied with our achievements when we're caught in the comparing trap.

When I joined the Harvard Business School faculty, I received cards and letters from friends and family congratulating me on achieving one of the ultimate "brass rings" of academics. I felt pretty good about myself until I visited my assigned office in Morgan Hall. In an adjacent office was a colleague who had written something like twelve books and was an internationally recognized scholar in the area of organizational innovation. He had a beautiful summer house near Cape Cod. In addition, he was gracious and supportive. There wasn't much to dislike. So every day I came to work and walked past his office door, I felt like I was behind in the race. Compared with my colleague, I had accomplished so little over such a long career; my two measly books were more like an embarrassment, given his output. When I passed his office and he wasn't there, I was sure that he was meeting with Jack Welch or someone famous. And as much as I wanted to dislike him, I found myself disliking *me* because of what he had done and what I had not accomplished. Mind you, this happened almost every day. And it didn't happen at the end of the day but at the beginning. I'm sure you are asking why I didn't just walk to my office from the other direction so I didn't have to begin the process of comparing? Because the situation on the other side was worse.

Two years earlier, in the mid-nineties, an MIT professor had joined the Harvard Business School faculty and one year later won the Nobel Prize in economics. Robert Merton was forty-six years old when he won the award. He and two other economists created the trading process called Black-Scholes that impacted the ways financial markets were informed and influenced. Now you see the problem. Merton had the office on the other side of my office. Bob Merton on one side of me, and Mike Tushman on the other. Bob Merton was as gracious and supportive as Mike Tushman. When I saw him driving to work, I would bristle. He would often wave; I couldn't figure out how someone that smart could be so gracious. So there you have it. There was no way for me to get to my office without a feeling of comparative inadequacy.

Comparing Without a Frame

A CEO who needed coaching contacted me. He ran a highly successful family-owned business. He was smart and gracious and committed to making the enterprise work. He was also aware of his blind spots and counterproductive patterns as a leader. When I began coaching him, he told me, "Tom, I met with this CEO and he told me to run my senior-level management team meetings a particular way. He also said to forget doing 360 reviews because they took up too much time and energy without any real payoff. Tom, should I do the same thing?" Another time, this client said another CEO he knew had told him that he spent 30 percent of his time in talent management reviews and coaching, and he wondered if he should do the same.

I appreciated the fact that my client was open to learning from other CEOs. But he would often issue edicts based on short conversations with other leaders that had far-reaching implications for the company. The organization would be creating a new technology system, then my CEO client would hear about another system from someone else and would respond by announcing that the whole company would be changing systems. His people were livid because they were asked to switch directions on a dime based on one conversation with another CEO—or with me. The employees felt whipsawed.

My client had confused learning with comparing. This happened repeatedly because he had never experienced any other organization than the organization he led. He had never had the chance to watch another CEO in action and learn from that observation. Consequently, he had to guess the right thing to do; fortunately, he guessed right a lot. However, at other times he struggled with the choices he faced and how he should allocate his time: "Do I visit country leaders or do I plan the next leadership development program for the first-line supervisors? Do I go and meet with the president of Company B or do I make policy on who can use the company fitness center?" Because my client lacked a frame—a range of experiences from which he could formulate his own theory of the case—he engaged in these comparing behaviors. As soon as someone he respected told him about a given method or strategy, he immediately began comparing what he and his company were doing versus the new approach. As a result, not only did this CEO fail to ground himself in his role, but his comparing behaviors made everyone else anxious about what they should be doing in their respective roles. You can imagine what the senior management team's decision-making process looked like. Essentially, this CEO's anxiety not only caused him to fall into the comparing trap, but also dragged his senior people along with him. Furthermore, the turnover rate for his senior team was far too high.

The lesson here that every high-need-for-achievement professional is: *Seek a range of experiences to avoid falling into the comparing trap.*

More specifically, don't settle into the routine that so many "comfortable" professionals settle into. Don't be content to just do your job. I'm not suggesting you have to work for ten different companies in ten years, but within your own organization, numerous opportunities exist for learning and growth. Volunteer for a team. Ask your boss for a stretch assignment. Spend time talking with people in other functions. Go to trade shows where you have the chance to meet people from other companies. Serve on internal or external (e.g., trade group) committees where you get to work with experts whom you ordinarily wouldn't get to work for.

Through formal and informal means, broaden your horizons. Narrow-minded professionals obsessively compare, since they automatically assume that they're missing out, that others have it better. With depth and breadth of experience, they are able to analyze their own situation more objectively rather than fantasize about what others have that they lack. When they see the world for what it is, they're less likely to be envious of scenarios that are largely of their own creation.

Real Benchmarks Versus False Measures

When Nitin Nohria, the current dean of the Harvard Business School, arrived as a new professor at the Harvard Business School in the late '80s, he tried to figure out the culture and expectations for success. He had done well studying at MIT and had multiple offers after graduation but decided to join the business faculty at Harvard. After a few short months, a professional relationship that was truly a mentor-apprentice model emerged. Professor Bob Eccles was a young tenured professor in the organizational behavior area. He too was white-hot smart, and gracious as well. Years later, when Nohria was tenured, had been senior associate dean, and had created a world-class reputation in academic circles, he related the following story about something Eccles had told him as he guided him early on.

As Eccles and Nohria walked through the parking lot of the School to their offices, Eccles asked Nohria to stop for a minute and then explained to him the following rules of engagement: "Nitin, I want you to look at this parking lot and let it be your guide as to your commitment to the school, your department, and your career. I want you to get here early enough in the morning so that you can park in the parking lot that is closest to school. As you know, it doesn't hold more than thirty cars. Second, I want you to stay at school long enough so that when you leave at night for home your car won't have any other cars around it. It will stick out like a beacon. If you follow this mantra you will be just fine."

This story illustrates the importance of establishing a handy benchmark to chart your professional progress rather than rely on false measures. Nohria had to write books, articles, and cases; be a good teacher; take on administrative duties; and create external relationships with research sites and other institutions. Yet it is often difficult to ascertain how well he was performing these roles and responsibilities. Enmeshed in the quotidian tasks of the job, it is easy to start wondering if another professor is a better teacher or writing more and better books. The trap of comparing is always there in a highly competitive yet ambiguous work environment, tempting people to fall victim to gnawing self-doubt by viewing their own accomplishments versus those of others. If Nohria ever forgot how to determine whether he was sufficiently engaged, an external measure existed for him to monitor whether he was measuring up. Eccles gave Nohria this advice only once, but he remembered it twenty years later, as well as the conversation's tone and context. Eccles had been around long enough to know what happened when someone didn't achieve "success" at the School and was asked to leave, and he had seen professors who had had their hearts set on making HBS their long-term professional career leave angry and bitter.

Eccles recognized that their failure to achieve their heart's desire from a career perspective was devastating and difficult to recover from. He didn't want Nohria to fall into the trap of comparing and fail to achieve his goal. Therefore, he gave him a simple way to assess if he was on the right track. By using the "parking lot factor" as his guide, he didn't have to resort to self-defeating comparing behaviors.

The parking-lot measure may not be appropriate for you, but I would urge you to find your own measure for providing a constant reminder that you're on track (or not) and help you avoid falling into the comparing behavior trap. And with the wrong person, certain measures may lead to busyness. Consider the following measures:

- Capstone progress: Chart your progress toward your ideal position, determining if you're acquiring the experiences and expertise that make you a viable candidate for that position.

- Satisfaction index: Keep track of how meaningful and fulfilling your work is; create a numerical satisfaction scale that
  depends on how much you're enjoying what you do and how
  purposeful it seems; take a reading regularly.

- Learning level: Assess the knowledge and skills you're acquiring and whether you're becoming an "expert" in any one area
  (this is a more subtle measure, but it still can serve as a viable
  alternative to comparing behaviors).

Introducing Jekyll and Hyde

It's not just in academia and business where professionals fall into the
comparing trap. All ambitious, driven people in just about every profession are ensnared by this reflex to judge themselves by what others
have done. For instance, a leader of a hospital requested my assistance
in dealing with a particular department in which the physicians didn't
get along. The acrimony had built up over time, and some members of
the department wouldn't speak to each other. My client asked,

> Tom, how can the most gifted doctors in the world not have
> the ability to work alongside one another? It's not that they are
> interpersonally incompetent. All of them can talk with their
> patients and the families of patients in an effective, empathic
> way. But once they get near their offices or the offices of other
> surgeons, it's as if they change from Jekyll to Hyde. World-
> class younger doctors don't want to come into the department
> because of the way they see the senior doctors treating one
> another. Recruiting has become an impossibility even though
> we have a great reputation. What advice do you have?

When I began to observe the respective doctors, even to the point
of observing surgeries, I realized that much of the anger was focused on

their figurative quest to become the highest-ranking doctor in the hospital. Obviously, there wasn't a real ranking of the doctors, but certain factors—number of successful surgeries, introduction of innovative techniques, publications, awards—all contributed to the status of each doctor within the hospital culture. Each doctor wanted to be number one in his own mind and in the minds of colleagues with whom he competed.

One day, as I walked down the hospital hallway near the surgical rooms, I saw a list of the surgeries planned for the day. Each of the surgeons had a certain number of scheduled procedures. When emergency cases arrived, an attending physician would assign the surgeries as fairly as possible. After each surgery, I noticed that surgeons would walk by the board and check off the surgery completed, then would run their eyes over the board and actually count the number of surgeries completed by the "competition." I asked one of the surgeons what he was studying as he looked at the board. He admitted, "I'm looking at who has performed the other surgeries, how long the surgery took to complete, and how difficult the procedure was." His last comment was said with a wry, tight grin.

All of these surgeons were highly skilled. I would have entrusted a relative who needed the kind of procedures these surgeons performed to any one of them. I respected them for their high level of technical skill. But their inability to turn off their need to compare and compete was destroying the department. Eventually, two of the best doctors left to join other very prestigious institutions. The president of the hospital tried a number of interventions to retain them but to no avail; too many doctors had already fallen deeply into the comparing trap.

Even the Best Leaders Can Be Trapped

It's not that high-need-for-achievement individuals can eliminate their comparing reflex completely, nor should they. Throughout history, our greatest generals, CEOs, lawyers, and other professionals have driven themselves to achieve significant objectives by trying to outdo others. Comparing becomes a trap, however, when people become so consumed by measuring themselves against others that they fail to step back and see how it's impacting their actions.

Even brilliant leaders fall victim to this trap. Ernest Shackleton was a wanderer and an explorer, and is perhaps best known today for preserving the lives of twenty-five men over an eighteen-month period on an expedition to the South Pole. The fact that he felt he was better at what he did than two other men in the "exploration business" grated on him night and day. Robert Peary seemed to be one step ahead of him in terms of finding places to discover. Peary had attempted to discover the North Pole, only to lose most of his men and almost die himself in the process. Peary was lauded, while Shackleton felt in his bones that at the end of the day Peary had failed in his efforts. Norway's Roald Amundsen also was world-famous for his ability to discover new lands and publicize his expeditions. Because of his comparing reflex, Shackleton was driven to put together a team of twenty-five men to walk across Antarctica.

The timing could not have been worse. World War I was beginning to take shape; all of Europe was tense. Shackleton desperately needed financial support, but there wasn't much to be had. Finally, he threw his materials together and headed for the South Pole. He made two stops in South America, one at South Georgia, on the tip of the continent, where there was a small whaling village. There a number of whalers told him there were more ice floes than usual. They warned Shackleton to beware of what might be coming his way.

Thirty miles from Antarctica and the starting point of his trek, his ship, the *Endurance*, was surrounded by ice and became stuck. Shackleton pulled off a miracle, keeping his crew alive over a year and a half of living on ice, floating in the stormy ocean in small boats, ending up on a rock-filled island, and finally getting back to South Georgia.

When he returned to England with every member of his crew alive, his entrance into the English harbor was met with a yawn. Everyone was focused on the war. While pulling off this miraculous adventure, he didn't achieve his goal of surpassing his two fellow explorers in terms of name recognition and acclaim.

So while comparing may have catalyzed his quest, it also may have prevented him from realizing his dream. If he had planned better, created a more viable strategy, and implemented it at the right time, he might have achieved his goal. Comparing, then, can create a trap that not only locks people into routines that prevent learning and growth but also causes them to pursue goals without sound strategies.

Comparing via Various Metrics

We measure ourselves against others in many different ways. As long as there are different metrics with which to compare our performance with others, we will be engaged in the process. A friend, for example, who runs a large hedge fund, complained to me not so long ago that he was miffed that he wasn't in the top ten money makers in the financial services arena. He had only made just over $125 million and there were others that had outpaced him. You see, we recalibrate at each higher level that we obtain. We redefine the game. And we always look up to reset the bar. Looking up is the only way we can continue reinforcing those traps that help us cover up our fundamental anxieties about who we are and how we are in the world.

When we keep upping the ante in our comparing behaviors, we can throw just about anything into the pot. Consider a partial list of what we use as a basis for comparison with others:

- Salary

- Bonuses

- Company performance

- Perks (access to company jets, stays at top hotels, golf junkets, luxurious office space, etc.)

- Vacations

- Houses, cars, boats

- Publicity (being on business magazine top 100 lists, flattering profiles, etc.)

- Reputation in industry

- Membership on boards

Go over this list and ask yourself when you've compared yourself in any of these categories with others in your company, your industry, or the business world in general. Then, reflect on your comparing behaviors and ask these questions:

- Did my comparing behaviors cause me to feel dissatisfied with my performance or my job? Did they take away from what otherwise were significant achievements?

- Did my comparing behaviors prevent me from achieving the goals that, with hindsight, I most wanted to achieve?

- Did my comparing behaviors cause me to expend a great deal of time and energy fretting about what I didn't possess rather than expend it on what I might accomplish?

While the most obvious form of comparing may be measuring your career progress against that of a peer, there are many others. While the most common negative consequence may involve never feeling satisfied with your achievements, there are other counterproductive effects.

Finally, I'd like to share a classic event that invites people to compare themselves with others: reunions. More specifically, I want to tell you about the Harvard Business School class reunion. Certainly people attend these reunions to see friends from the past. But there is another reason they come back: to judge how they have done relative to their colleagues. As a faculty member who is invited to speak at the events, I have noticed that the younger the alumni reunion class is, the more comparing that takes place. In fact, I will no longer speak at the five-year reunion—it's too hard to create discussions that are in-depth and reflective with all the comparing that goes on.

Those alumni back for the five-year reunions are guarded, wear just a little too much makeup and cologne, and are generally adopting invulnerable poses. This makes it difficult if not impossible for them to relax and confess that there have been bumps in the road. There is much more talk about when they get their first payout or how many square feet they have in their new homes or where they are going on vacation. I ran into one graduate who was scheduled to attend her five-year reunion but had just been laid off. When I saw her I asked her if she planned on attending the reunion. She blushed and looked cornered. She then confessed that it was too stressful—there was no way she could attend not having a job.

When I responded that no one there cared too much about such a detail because they were too concerned about themselves, she became dismissive. She replied, "You just don't understand. I lived with these people for two years. While they will act supportive, they will think that I haven't made it. It will reinforce their views of me because I wasn't one of the smartest students in the class." I smiled and told her that there would be others who didn't feel as though they had been successful. But I realized my words of support were falling on deaf ears. I wondered after my brief interaction with this former student whether only those who saw themselves as successes showed up to the reunions. If that were true, no wonder the conversations were more shallow and superficial than those of the alumni who were older and wiser and who had fallen off their career paths more than once.

On the other hand, when I facilitated discussions with alumni who had been gone for twenty-five years, they jumped into deeper conversation, much more willing to discuss their lives, successes, and challenges. My colleague Leslie Perlow and I wrote selected profiles of alumni from 1976 to use as case studies in the first-year curriculum on organizational behavior. The first time we taught these six stories, we were blown away by how much commotion was created.

The students thought we had intentionally selected six alumni who had had particularly troubled lives as reference points. When we told them that they were selected from a stratified random sample, they were shocked. There had been two divorces, a child born with learning disabilities, the death of a spouse. The students reported that they left the classroom not encouraged by the future but discouraged and depressed. They were comparing their dreams with the realities of alumni who had lived full but flawed lives. These current students had envisioned some smooth path to capstone positions and great personal satisfaction. The reality was that the six alumni we profiled, though highly accomplished in certain ways, had also experienced a variety of setbacks and problems.

The lesson: you can fall victim to comparisons with impossible dreams. I'm not suggesting that you refrain from dreaming, only that you don't become discouraged because your dreams may not match up with other people's realities. No doubt, our students saw themselves twenty-five years from that moment and were disheartened. This is an insidious form of comparing, and it can cause people to lose their drive and their dreams if they're not careful. Your dreams can obviously make you, but they can also destroy you. You may settle for less and never open yourselves up to all the possibilities and the risks a truly great life requires.

Now let's move on to the next trap: *blaming*.

CHAPTER EIGHT

Blame

How Can I Convince Others That It's Their Fault?

V ERY SMART, ACCOMPLISHED, high-need-for-achievement professionals find it difficult to hear that they haven't met expectations.
The internal dialogue is, "I've worked so hard, how can anyone criticize my work?" They don't want to hear that someone can do it better
or has done it better at some point in the past. These ambitious, driven
professionals take these matters personally. It's not just business. As a
result, they find it difficult to accept that they may have fallen short in
some area and need to change their attitudes or behaviors in order to
do better the next time. Instead of making themselves vulnerable by
saying "mea culpa," they say, "It's not my fault; it's his!"

If you find yourself pointing your finger at others frequently, recognize that you are falling into the trap of *blaming others*.

FIGURE 8-1

Problem-solving curve

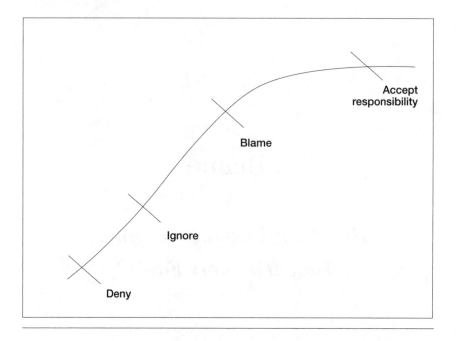

Figure 8-1 illustrates how the problem-solving curve works, and in so doing reveals how we fall into the blaming trap. When we believe we have disappointed someone else and, more important, ourselves, we deny a problem exists; this is how the process starts. After we deny, we then ignore the problem for as long as possible. Once the situation is just too obvious and too painful to ignore, we transfer the problem to someone else. This is the stage in which we often become stuck for an extended period of time. We find creative ways to rationalize our behavior and stick it on someone else. We demonize the other person to avoid seeing ourselves in a negative light.

If you recall the four quadrants introduced in chapter 2 (figure 2-2), you'll see how the problem-solving curve prevents high-need-for-achievement professionals from changing, learning and growing;

more specifically, how the curve keeps returning them to the quadrant where they do the wrong thing well.

Consider Jack, a fast-track software executive who has capitalized on his technology expertise and his business acumen to become one of the youngest vice presidents in his large software company's history. At thirty-five, Jack has hopped from one position to the next and turned in stellar performances consistently. Even when he's encountered problems in the past, he's found ways around them using his considerable knowledge and skills.

Jack is assigned responsibility for the team that's introducing a new software product with tremendous market potential—it's based on a revolutionary technology that competitors lack, and Jack's company has invested heavily in it. Jack is confident in his ability to lead his team in the product's successful introduction. Things go well initially as the team formulates market and distribution strategies, marketing, and so on. The first glitch occurs during a beta test when a significant percentage of the products fail to perform effectively. At first, Jack adopts his typically aggressive problem-solver approach, providing motivation and technical insight to help his team deal with the design flaw. But the problem persists despite his team's tweaks to the design, and frustration sets in. Shortly thereafter, a competitor introduces a similar product based on a different technology, beating Jack's company to the market.

Jack's bosses are furious and place tremendous pressure on him to fix the design error and get the product to market as quickly as possible. Yet there are further delays, and when the company CEO calls Jack into his office and says that Jack has let him down, Jack protests that it is not his fault but that of the three designers who had primary responsibility for the product, claiming, "I'm only human" and "I believed the information they gave me." What Jack doesn't say is that he took on this project without making the effort to understand the product's technology fully; that he felt "dumb" when he started asking people questions about it and hated how he felt; and that he decided that he really didn't need to know the technology "at a grassroots level" and would just trust his people. Perhaps even more alarmingly, Jack's people *did* inform him early on that there might be a potential issue with the design and that it would be wise to consider some alternatives, but Jack was so intent on delivering the product on time that he brushed aside their concerns. Though the team eventually got the design right and introduced the product with moderate success, Jack requested reassignment to a team that was working on a project in his sweet spot—he knew the technology and the market thoroughly. Still, for months afterward, Jack continued to blame the designers for the blemish on his record.

Like many ambitious professionals, Jack couldn't use this problem-solving experience to learn and grow. He couldn't tolerate the vulnerability he felt when things didn't go according to plan—his plan. He was unable to accept blame and the reflection and self-assessment that come with it. Instead of learning, changing, and growing as a result of the experience, Jack returned to the comfortable quadrant of doing the wrong thing well.

Return to the problem-solving curve for a moment. Recognize that it takes considerable time to move to the point in this curve where we accept appropriate responsibility. We must be brave enough to own up to our role without personalizing the problem and experiencing shame. From this frame of mind we can move to the problem-solving stage and action focus. This is where we begin to see that this discomfort won't kill us. We start to recognize that we can and will survive our vulnerability, and that we don't have to blame others.

Attribution Error: I Am So Sensitive, and You Are So Not

At this point, you may be thinking to yourself, "Okay, I may compare and I may cling to a busy schedule, but blaming is one trap I don't fall into."

If you possess a mind-set similar to most high-need-for-achievement types, you find it difficult to admit that you would be so callow as to blame others for your own shortcomings. In fact, many professionals I know are brilliant at rationalizing away their blaming behaviors. Consciously, they're convinced they're in the right; subconsciously, they recognize that blaming helps them keep their anxiety at bay.

Let's take a closer look at what goes on in the minds of hard-driving professionals who succumb to this blaming reflex. Specifically, if these professionals were able to be honest with themselves and assess why they pointed a finger at someone else when things went wrong, here's what they might say: "I feel exposed or worried about my internal survival, and even though these worries may be absurd or exaggerated, they cause me to exaggerate the differences between myself and others. I am smarter, savvier, and more sensitive than my colleagues, so I am inherently less likely to have been at fault than those other people. I widen the differences between myself and others as I find additional ways to blame others for negative outcomes."

Consider how we filter information based on the differences we see between ourselves and others. Here's what I've found myself doing. I give myself the benefit of the doubt because I know my inner feelings and intentions. Simultaneously, I see only the surface behavior of someone else and judge the person accordingly. I judge others by what I observe. I subsequently create my own rationale of their behavior based on my thoughts and feelings, not on theirs: *John recommended that we stick with our strategy because he's afraid to take a risk, unlike me who has the best interests of the company at heart and will take whatever risks are necessary to help the company prosper. Furthermore, John seems to be angling for a promotion, so right now he probably is saying what he's saying to avoid making a career mistake. I would never do that; I know I would be willing to take a career step backward for the sake of the company; others aren't as noble and self-sacrificing as I am.*

Most of us believe we have perfected the art of knowing the motivation, intention, and true feelings of others, when in reality we are often clueless, our biased filters skewing our perception. I see my behavior is caused by the external context, and I judge your behavior using my ability to intuit your thoughts and feelings. Thus, I am quick to blame because I am so insightful and sensitive to others.

Most high achievers believe they possess great empathy. One colleague said, "I know that everyone thinks he is extra sensitive to others, just like all men think they are superb drivers. But in all seriousness, I really *do* think that one of my strengths is understanding others and knowing what they are thinking and feeling." When I tell this story in large groups of professionals, I always hear rueful laughter—people immediately recognize themselves.

I've experienced the same sense of recognition at times. Even as a little kid running around the streets of Portland, Oregon, I began to think that I was special and that others were naturally drawn to me because of who I was. As I became older, I assumed my special quality was that I was extra sensitive to the needs of others. My older brother Kurt knew I believed this about myself, and he put my feelings in perspective when he said, "Tom, you often tell me that your journey through life is tougher because you experience others so deeply and pick up on their pain. Well, most people would say the same thing. Most people think they are especially gifted in understanding others. So know that you can go along and think that you have special powers, but so do I, and most everyone else thinks they do as well."

Garrison Keillor, author and producer of *Prairie Home Companion*, talking about his own motivations and fears, said, "I have always been frightened of living an ordinary life. I was homely as a kid (and still am) and had no friends growing up. I was tall and awkward and worried what I would do with my life. It wasn't until college that I realized I had a voice that caught people's attention. I was on to something. I also realized that I could write. Now, as I reflect on my life I've realized that we are all worried of living the ordinary life, of making no difference at all. But what I've come to understand is that the ordinary life is good enough."[1]

Our fears of being ordinary combined with our sense of being extraordinarily sensitive souls prompt us to seek scapegoats when things go wrong in our work lives. By refusing to accept blame, we protect ourselves from our concern that we're just regular Joes and Joans who are prone to making mistakes. By finding someone else to take the fall when things go bad, we preserve our belief that we possess some special insight into other people's internal flaws. We're especially likely to subscribe to these beliefs when our careers are losing traction or things are going wrong for us in other ways at work. In addition, many of us find it easier to blame others rather than ourselves because we have inflated views of our impact on the world and on others. We give ourselves the benefit of the doubt because we know that we are genuine and earnest; we couldn't be at fault; the fault must lie with Mark, who is less genuine, or Mary, who is less earnest than we are.

A Culture of Finger-Pointing

Professor Scott Snook of the Harvard Business School researched extensively in his book, *Friendly Fire: The Accidental Shootdown of U.S. Black Hawks over Northern Iraq*, why the phenomenon of *friendly fire*—when individuals from the same military group accidentally harm one another during combat—happens in war. On April 14, 1994, after the first Iraqi war, the U.S. military was part of a multicountry force to protect the Kurdish people in Northern Iraq. Saddam Hussein had killed nearly five hundred thousand Kurds over a five-year period. An allied "coordinated" military force enforced a no-fly zone over Northern Iraq over Kurdish territory, but in the process of carrying out this assignment, U.S. Air Force F-15s accidentally shot down two U.S. Black Hawk helicopters while an AWACS (Air Warning and Control System) plane watched this incident unfold, high above the accident at thirty-five thousand feet. Twenty-six people, military and civilian personnel riding in the helicopter who were on a peacekeeping mission, were killed in a flash—twenty minutes from start to finish. Investigation of the accident uncovered a number of mistakes made that day by different parties. Brigadier General Jeffrey S. Pilkington, who was in charge of all military actions in the NFZ, gave permission for the two Black Hawks to fly into the zone without informing anyone they were going to be there. The AWACS officers observing in the area failed to inform the F-15 pilots that the Black Hawks were friendly aircraft. The F-15 pilots failed to identify the Black Hawks as friendly aircraft. Finally, the IFF Code (identification system used to identify enemy aircraft) was not coordinated into the overall defense system.

Errors were made on an individual, team, overall organizational, and systems levels. But when the dust cleared, only one U.S. officer was held accountable for the accident, Captain James Wang of the U.S. Air Force. Many felt that Captain Wang was a scapegoat and that General Pilkington should have been prosecuted, since he was responsible for the overall operation. The finger-pointing continues to this day. No one stepped up and accepted responsibility. No one said, "Yes, I made a mistake. You should hold me accountable for this disaster." All parties involved in the incident spent their time and energy blaming others. The attribution error was played out on multiple levels.

When I teach this case to highlight organizational misalignment, every leader in the audience relates to it. They all say, "That reminds me of our organization. That could be us. Just change the title on the story. We are an accident waiting to happen."

In organizations, people are loath to accept blame and quick to point fingers. While many leaders make a great show of "accepting responsibility," they tend to do so in name only. They say, "I was responsible," but they fire others, not themselves. Even more commonly, many high achievers deflect attention from their mistakes and focus the spotlight on the mistakes others have made. As in the friendly fire case, the guilty parties are usually multiple rather than singular. No doubt, it wasn't just one person at Toyota who was the cause of the company's recent woes resulting in a massive recall. If everything comes out in the wash, it will turn out that a variety of people at a variety of levels in a variety of positions contributed to the mess. It takes a great deal of courage and a willingness to step forward and admit an error, and when you've been acculturated to the concept of "plausible deniability" and maintaining a perfect record, then showing that courage can be difficult.

Determine the extent that your culture encourages finger-pointing and discourages taking responsibility for mistakes. To that end, consider these questions:

- Have you or any of your colleagues been disciplined or fired for admitting a mistake?

- Do your senior leaders preach accountability but rarely admit mistakes themselves? Do they ever punish themselves for mistakes by not taking a bonus, not giving themselves a raise, or enduring embarrassment by going public with their errors?

- Do managers routinely push blame down to lower levels? Do they seek to find convenient scapegoats who lack the clout to defend themselves?

- Do subordinates consistently pay for the sins of bosses who are less than effective?

If your answers suggest a culture of blame, it might behoove you to look for work in cultures with different values. While a blaming reflex exists in many cultures, it's a reflex that exists on a continuum. What you need to determine is how prevalent the blaming is. Does it happen all the time or infrequently? Does a manager blame a direct report for a mistake in the heat of the moment but apologize later and accept part or all of the blame?

Ideally, you'll be able to accept blame with impunity in your culture. Therefore, try it! Test the culture by making a conscious effort to confess your culpability for a small mistake (assuming you bear some responsibility for the mistake)—maybe it's a late shipment, a glitch in a presentation, a missed appointment. It's nothing major, but it's significant enough that the mistake causes some consternation. If your culture is sufficiently forgiving, your admission of fault won't result in punishment of any kind. Your boss won't chew you out; your colleagues won't treat you as incompetent. In fact, in strong cultures, your admission will have a positive impact. You'll be seen as honest and open. You will be viewed as having the courage to admit when you were wrong.

Obviously, you don't want to make mistakes all the time and be constantly confessing your shortcomings. But it's often the case that admitting your shortcomings is liberating—it liberates you from the blame trap. When you say you were wrong, you make yourself vulnerable. And what you learn is that being vulnerable is not as horrible as you might have imagined. In fact, it can be a relief. Gaining practice in being vulnerable on small things is a prelude to being vulnerable on a larger scale—a prerequisite for doing the right thing poorly.

How Blame Shields Us from Our Flaws

If you'll recall the first chapter's profile of high-need-for-achievement professionals, you'll understand why this blaming trap is so appealing to this group. Psychologically, it offers a temporary but remarkably effective blindfold to our flaws. When we're so used to thinking of ourselves as the best of the best, it's enormously difficult to swallow our pride and admit that we made mistakes. As much as we may grasp on some level that we blundered and as much as we may feel it's right to confess that blunder, our self-image won't allow it. We would prefer to keep our pristine, though false, reputation for mistake-free managing intact rather than admit error. Blame is a way we can fool others as well as ourselves. When we convince one and all that the fault lies elsewhere, we can maintain our illusion that we're as competent and insightful as we've been told we have to be to succeed in a highly competitive arena.

To counteract this illusion, root your blaming behavior in a specific experience. Think about an incident that occurred in your group when a big problem blew up and everyone was upset about it. Choose an incident in which your initial response was to lash out at someone else, when with hindsight you realized you bore at least some of the responsibility. Then use these questions to assess the underlying psychology of the finger-pointing:

- Did you truly believe that you were free from guilt for the mistake that was made? At the time that heat was pouring down from management and you felt the pressure, did you dismiss your involvement in creating some aspect of the problem and focus on who was *really* responsible?

- With hindsight, think about the individual or individuals you singled out for blame. Why did you choose them—were they sufficiently low on the totem pole that you could lay into them without consequences, or did you choose them because you felt guilty for not supervising them properly or not listening to their warnings?

- As soon as the incident occurred, did you consider saying something to the effect of, "I was involved in this project, and if anyone should be blamed, I should be; others may have contributed to the problem, but if I had done x, y, or z, I could have prevented it." When you think about making such a statement, what fears does it raise?

Admittedly, these are tough questions for high-need-to-achieve professionals to ask, but you need to surface the issues in order to address them. You need to be aware of how and why your impulse to blame arises. More important, you need to grasp that while this blaming may provide a temporary balm, it will invariably be destructive to your career as well as to your effectiveness.

To get this point across, I want to share a nonbusiness story, one that involves a close friend who talked to me about the gradual dissolution of his marriage. Chad had been married for twenty-five years. The youngest of his three boys had just left for college, and Chad couldn't fathom what he and his spouse would do as empty nesters, without the kids in the home. Over time he began to find reasons why he saw the world differently from Ann, his wife, and these reasons became his rationale for why he should leave the marriage. Chad said that the more he thought about these reasons, the more he became convinced that it was Ann's fault the marriage didn't work. As he moved toward the divorce, Chad would reflect on his failings as a husband, but concluded that he played only a minor role—that her flaws were more responsible for the marriage's demise than his own. Years after the divorce, Chad said, "I think I was so scared about ending the relationship, I think I was so embarrassed that I couldn't keep it together or perhaps didn't want to, that I created a bulletproof story. I think I needed to build up courage to act on something so monumental and out of my realm of possibility that I filtered everything through blame. As I think about it now, I see that I played a key role in the divorce as well."

If Chad had had this insight earlier, might it have preserved his marriage? If he had understood that he was guilty of blaming to preserve his own self-image, would he have learned the lessons that would help him in other relationships? While it's impossible to know what would have happened, I'm sure Chad wished he had blamed less and accepted more of the responsibility for the marriage's problems. Though it was too late for Chad, it's not too late for high-need-for-achievement professionals who are constantly looking for others to take the fall.

Alternatives to Blaming

To avoid or escape the blaming trap, you must have options when the opportunity arises to blame someone for mistakes. In other words, if you possess alternatives to yelling at a subordinate or scapegoating an innocent but convenient target, you're likely to choose one of them. In this way, your anxiety might translate into productive rather than unproductive actions; you may sidestep this trap and allow yourself to feel vulnerable and uncertain and take a chance on changing.

But I'm getting ahead of myself. Let's concentrate on three alternatives when you find yourself wanting to blame someone:

- Have a nonaccusatory, constructive conversation with your candidate for blame.

- Rely on a mentor or expert to help analyze what went wrong and why.

- Confess your sins privately.

You'll notice that public confession isn't on the list. While this is a great alternative that I would encourage you to consider, I recognize that it may be a difficult leap for some highly ambitious, perfectionist professionals.

Setting The Bar Too High

Do you sometimes feel as if you can never meet the expectations others have for you or that you have for yourself? In fact, you probably can't meet these expectations because they're absurdly high. As a high-need-for-achievement individual, you've set ambitious goals for yourself. That's fine. But there's a difference between ambitious goals and unrealistic ones. Some people are set on making their first $1 billion before age forty or becoming CEO of a *Fortune* 500 company before age fifty. When you fixate on unrealistic goals and fail to achieve them, you become bitter and cynical. Instead of resetting your goals realistically, you take out your disappointment on others. You blame others for failing to choose you for the top spot.

I would bet that more than 50 percent of the conversations among ambitious professionals in workplaces involve blaming: the CEO for being a mediocre leader, the customer for being disloyal, the boss for being moody, the direct report for being lazy. These blaming conversations are especially prevalent when colleagues get together for lunch, coffee, or drinks and feel less constrained about issuing complaints.

The conversations often go along these lines: "You know, Bill is a great guy and is really committed to the firm. He works very hard—but he really ought to talk more with us about the direction of the firm. And even if he has this interest in creating a national footprint, every firm wants to do the same. And it would be really great if he dealt with those partners in the firm who aren't bringing in new clients and just don't bill that many hours anymore; they are good people but take away from the productive culture we are known for. Bill spends a lot of time traveling to the other offices, but what does he do when he's there? Don't you think his time could be better spent focusing on our major clients and generating new business? And what about his successor? I don't think he has given the firm that many options on future leaders because he hasn't got many younger professionals to choose from."

The topic of these conversations always returns to a critique of the firm or company leaders or a description of the inefficiencies of the other partners. And at the end of each evening, as these colleagues leave the bar, they are weary not only by the day's events but also by the unproductive conversation they have just had. They get worn down by the blaming and the criticizing and the ongoing cynicism that emerges through these counterproductive dialogues.

When we complain about people who fall short, our own failings fade into the background. We have learned that it's easier and more fun to talk about others' shortcomings rather than grapple with how we can improve a performance evaluation system or how we might restructure a group to make it more effective. We prefer to gossip about other people's bad moves rather than examine what we might do differently.

We demand far too much from our leaders, our colleagues, and our direct reports because we demand too much from ourselves. We set expectations that we can't meet, and we rationalize (albeit subconsciously) that others should not be exempt from these absurdly high expectations. Thus, we set up people to take the blame when things don't go according to plan.

If you have fallen into this particular blaming trap, the remedy is to make a conscious effort to set realistic expectations for yourself and your colleagues. More specifically:

- Handicap your expectations; determine the odds of achieving your key career goals so that you know if a goal is realizable or if it's more wishful thinking than reality.

- Reset your expectations based on the odds; focus on goals where you have at least a 50-50 chance of achieving them.

- Assess what you expect of others—bosses, colleagues, direct reports—and their odds of achieving objectives; figure out

what is fair to expect of them given their experience, expertise, and situation; if you determine that you expect too much,
scale down your expectations so that they have a good chance
of meeting them.

Please don't misunderstand the previous exercise. I'm not suggesting that you should not expect much of yourself and others. Expecting
too little of yourself and your colleagues is just as bad as expecting
too much. It's always good to set goals where you need to stretch to
achieve them. But stretching isn't the same as quantum leaps. When
you find the sweet spot between overly ambitious and underwhelming
goals, you're much less likely to blame others when things go awry.

I Really Am Smarter Than You

When I was at Morgan Stanley, a colleague and I disagreed on whether
we should hire another investment banker at a senior level. I was in-
sistent that it wasn't a good idea. My friend thought it was an excellent idea. Eventually the leaders in the investment banking division
decided to go ahead with the hire. There was much celebration in the
division because we had "stolen" a key banker whom we needed in a
particular area of the business. I was not thrilled. I had lost the skir-
mish. I had argued hard in dissent and was outvoted.

What is embarrassing as I look back on the whole incident is that
from the day this new star hire joined the organization, I acted distant
and aloof from him. I didn't go out of my way to make him feel as if he
was now part of the firm. I assumed that those who were so excited
to have him would embrace him and socialize him into the firm. Three
months after he was hired, I heard rumblings that this banker hadn't
delivered on some clients who were supposed to follow him to our firm
accounts. I remember attending a partner dinner to which he was invited but didn't show. Six months into this relationship, he went back

to the firm where he had been for fifteen years. His sponsors were shocked, and I'm sure embarrassed, that they had invested so much without reaping any benefits.

The first thought I had immediately after I had heard the news was, "I told you so. I knew this would happen. I told you this would be the outcome before he ever joined." I find myself feeling embarrassed and ashamed as I write this, but it's the truth. I blamed the sponsors that it didn't work out. I blamed the professional himself for not working hard enough to make the situation work. But of course, I didn't blame myself. Upon reflection, I think I actually sabotaged the lateral hire because it was more important for me to prove myself right—to look smarter than the others. It was more important for me to be seen a seer, as an insightful guru who could read people and the future and know what would play out before it ever did. It was more important for me to be right and prove others wrong, and to blame them. I could have chastised myself for being too prideful to help socialize this new person into the firm; I could have taken a long, hard look at why I remained distant from him rather than helping him contribute his considerable knowledge and skills to the enterprise. But I did not.

The lesson: when we blame others for being "stupid" about something, we are able to portray ourselves as smarter than they are. High-need-to-achieve professionals often feel the need to be smarter than others to prove their own worth. In fact, they are often only smarter in their own minds; by telling themselves that their colleagues are dense, slow, and unperceptive, they elevate their own business intelligence. They are, of course, fooling no one with this blaming trick except themselves.

Finding Blame-Free Organizational Zones

Ideally, you work for an organization where specific policies mitigate against blaming behaviors. You might recall my story from chapter 4 about John Mackey, chairman of Whole Foods Markets, who requires a unanimous vote from all department members approving a new hire; this policy helps avoid scapegoating the newest member of a team if things go wrong.

Another company with blame-free policies is Egon Zehnder International, the international executive search firm. For instance, a job applicant goes through anywhere from twenty-five to forty interviews, and everyone needs to vote affirmatively. The same practice was used by Jack Rifkin who created the world's most dominant equities research department at Lehman Brothers. Rifkin spent a high percentage of his time ensuring that all new hires had the commitment of everyone on the team. The two professionals who would be sitting on each side of the new hire each received two votes. They were key in helping the person succeed in the new position. There was no blame in those groups. When problems emerged or mistakes were made, the individuals were more courageous and honest in stepping up and taking responsibility. Many times, the whole group would take ownership for goals not achieved.

Even if you don't work for companies with organization-wide policies such as these, you should at least try to find a group within a company in which blame is not a chronic way of interacting with others. Look for a boss who accepts responsibility for mistakes, if not all the time then some of the time. Search for teams or other groups in which, after mistakes are made, people talk more about what they can do differently next time to avoid these mistakes rather than perseverating about who is to blame. Perhaps most important of all, seek groups that demonstrate a certain tolerance for error—in other words, the boss and other group members recognize that small mistakes are the price you pay for learning. These groups don't want people to mess up, but they recognize that it's a natural part of the work process and therefore don't beat up professionals who make the occasional error.

Like busyness and comparing, blame is a trap we set for ourselves to cover up the anxieties that drive us to do what we do, act how we act, and be the kind of person we may not want to be. All three of these traps are serious stuff, but there's one more trap you should know about, and it has become the most enticing and devastating trap of them all. In some ways, it lays the foundation for the other three traps. I'm talking about *worry*.

CHAPTER NINE

Worry

I Know There Is a Crisis
Waiting for Me

JANA WAS A SUCCESSFUL, EXPERIENCED MANAGER who had run a multimillion-dollar business. She projected the image of being able to do it all. She was COO of an Internet consulting firm and had previously run a major piece of a large consulting firm. Decisive, energetic, smart, driven, and with a wonderful family, she seemingly had it made. Her managerial style, however, did not suggest someone who had everything going for her. Instead, it revealed a high-need-for-achievement professional who had fallen into the *worrying* trap—constant, counterproductive fretting about how a given decision or event would turn out.

Jana's anxiety-ridden managerial style made others nervous. In good times and bad, she worried, and she shared her worries with others. She was a master at turning any positive possibility into five potential negative outcomes. After an interaction, her subordinates left more anxious than before the interaction began. Colleagues often remarked that they avoided walking by her office because they could *feel* her worry.

Her horizon always seemed ominous; there was some disaster visible in the distance and approaching fast. One colleague lamented, "Every time I had what I thought was a good idea or an alternative way of looking at a problem, Jana would convince me that my idea could cause the downfall of the company. After a while I realized it would be better just to wait until I had a bunch of people on board before I tried to convince her otherwise." Even Jana reflected, "I wouldn't know how to be any other way than to worry about everything. From my daughter's school, to my husband's job, to my son's orthodontia, to this business. That's just the way I am. And at some level I know that I can make others anxious when I worry too much."

Jana isn't unique. We live and work in an age when there is plenty to fret about for professionals in every field and at every level. This worrying becomes a trap, however, when we start seeing doom and gloom everywhere, when it colors our decision making and behaviors, when it causes us to go into a shell or always respond in the same tried-and-true ways to avoid catalyzing our worst fears. We all worry. But Jana, like many driven professionals today, often worries needlessly, excessively, and counterproductively. While a moderate amount of worry may focus the mind, too much diminishes effectiveness and robs us of our ability to move outside our comfort zone (because there is even more to worry about outside of that zone!).

Worry About the Right Stuff

After thirty years of observing various leaders, a consultant friend noted this irony: leaders worry too much about the obvious. Of course, they should worry about compensation and where the organization is going, about departments and divisions and whether they are making money. What they don't worry about is what their people are worried about: whether they have purpose in the organization; whether they are part of the team (isolation); whether they matter and their work matters (significance).

Reflect on how you feel when your concerns about significance, isolation, and purpose aren't addressed. If you're like most driven professionals, your anxieties spiral out of control and become a trap. Instead of feeling sufficiently secure and confident in your work, you are so consumed by worry that you have great difficulty trying something new or innovative. You cleave to your routines in an effort to minimize that worry or at least avoid any negative consequences that might send these worries into the stratosphere. You feel you don't have anyone to talk to about what you're worried about, and so these unarticulated fears gain power over you. No one expresses gratitude for what you do. No one offers affirmation. No one helps you confront your worries and get them out in the open. Think about what work worries assault you in the middle of the night and prevent you from going back to sleep. Use the following questions to help bring worries to the surface:

- Do you suspect that you are nothing more than an interchangeable part?

- Do you feel separated from the core of the company and feel like your office is an island?

- Do you fear that you have lost what drove you to excel when you first joined the company, and now you don't know the larger reason why you work there?

- Do you worry that you've fallen out of favor with your boss?

- Do you believe that your work is no longer of the quality that it once was?

- Do you think that your people talk about your failings behind your back and think you're a poor manager or producer?

- Do you worry that a senior manager, a customer, or someone else has it in for you?

My Office Isn't Large Enough

Some high-need-for-achievement professionals worry about big things—whether to go forward with an acquisition that can make or break the company, whether to downsize the workforce, whether to make a major career change. But the worry that can trap these professionals often exists on a smaller scale, a relatively minor matter that grows in its power to bedevil and bewilder. Someone once said that there are no small worries for people with big ambition, since every obstacle on the road to goals looms large. To help you understand how insidious small worries can be, let me tell you about Nicole.

She was a manager who was deeply and disturbingly worried about office space. Nicole, equally gifted at managing her team and dealing with clients, had become one of the youngest office heads of one of the larger financial services firms, specializing in private wealth management. When looking at some research her staff had compiled about prospective clients in Los Angeles (where the office was located), Nicole recognized that an opportunity existed to bring in more Korean high-net-wealth clients. The problem was that her group had no Korean professionals, and she decided that it would be a good idea to recruit one. The search was lengthy and extensive. She finally hired John, who was of Korean descent and seemingly had the confidence and background to break into this market.

As John was socializing into the new office, he began to act edgy and a bit out of sorts. Eventually, the other office professionals began distancing themselves from him. It became clear to Nicole that John didn't really fit in. Then he brought in six big accounts in less than two months. Even those who didn't connect with John celebrated, since his sales reflected well on the team. One week after making these sales, John asked Nicole if he could have a bigger office. He said that, to be successful in his new job, he needed to demonstrate his importance to clients. During the conversation, John implied that if Nicole didn't grant his request, competing firms would. Nicole didn't know what to do, and for three days, she agonized about this choice. She felt at heart that doing what John requested wasn't fair to the other professionals who had been there for a number of years and also deserved larger offices; she also didn't like his veiled threat. On the other hand, John was turning into an office star who was carrying out her mission to bring in more affluent Korean clients. More specifically, Nicole wondered if she really understood John and his cultural heritage and values.

Nicole worried to the point of insomnia at night and headaches during the day as she tried to make the decision. She was unable to compartmentalize her problems and focus on whatever she was doing. She had other important managerial decisions to make, but she found that as hard as she tried to deal with these other matters, the issue of John wanting a bigger office intruded. It wasn't just that she debated the pros and cons of whether to grant John's request. It's that her initial worry spiraled into other worries: if she gave John the office he wanted, she might offend Joe and Laurie, who had been her best people over the years; they might leave and go to other firms; or the morale might sink so low that the group would no longer function as an effective team; or it just wouldn't be as fun to work in the group because of the poor morale. On the other side of the coin, if she were to deny John's request, Nicole worried that he might leave the firm; that if he left, the group's results would be much less robust; that management would be upset with her for allowing John to leave; and that maybe she wasn't really cut out to be a manager since she hated making these types of decisions.

Nicole's worries turned into a web of interconnected concerns, fears, and general anxiety. She was unable to extricate herself as she went about her daily tasks, postponing the decision and dragging out the worry for another few days, then another week. She began to see parallels with other issues she had confronted during her tenure as a manager, issues that caused her to become enmeshed in a thicket of nettlesome thoughts and distracted her from more pressing issues. Nicole also realized that these worries caused her to hunker down and avoid doing much of anything. It seemed to her that she just couldn't handle one more problem or deal with one more challenge, and so she avoided decisions, postponed implementing approved programs, and was skittish about any task that was new and unfamiliar.

Like many managers, Nicole had allowed worry to segue from a catalyst to a trap. A certain amount of worry helped her achieve tangible goals, but it became counterproductive when she confronted more amorphous goals and less measurable outcomes. Ambiguity, paradox, and uncertainty all caused Nicole's worries to move into this counterproductive territory, and though she was aware that it was happening, she had no idea what she might do about it.

However, there are three things that you can do about this worry trap:

- First, "box up" your small worry so that it doesn't spread. Nicole allowed her worry to infect other areas of her work life; her worries about John caused her to start worrying about other direct reports; in turn, these concerns caused her to question her own judgment and whether she was slipping. To avoid this spreading worry, make a conscious effort to confine your fears and anxieties to the subject at hand. There's a term in pop psychology circles called *stinking thinking*, and it essentially means that people allow their thoughts to run away in negative and often illogical directions. Don't let that happen in these situations. Instead, keep reminding yourself that a problem in one area does not mean that there's a problem in another area. Keep returning your focus to the specific issue, and recognize when you're allowing your worry to spread in illogical and unproductive directions.

- Second, make a specific agenda and specific tasks associated with the agenda so that you are less likely to distract yourself with a less critical issue.

- Third, address the issue causing the worry quickly and decisively. I know this isn't always easy, especially for high-need-for-achievement personalities who can analyze an issue to death. Nicole should have decided to give John his office right away or decided not to give it to him. Even if her decision had produced negative consequences, they probably would not have been nearly as negative as being caught in the worry trap. Increasingly, professionals in positions of responsibility are facing right-versus-right decisions—there is no perfect answer. Or they're facing wrong-versus-wrong decisions—either choice is going to have unpleasant repercussions. In these instances, you have to call a halt to your analysis and rely on your instincts to see you through. Trust your gut rather than be caught in the indecisive middle.

Speak More and Watch the Conversation Fade into Oblivion

Worry is a trap in more ways than one. Perhaps the most subtle, yet serious impact of being consumed by worry is that it impacts the conversations you have with colleagues, customers, and other stakeholders.

Communication is crucial for learning, growth, and change; it is also essential if you hope to derive meaning and fulfillment from work experiences. Yet worry corrupts conversations, making it less effective and satisfying than it should be.

If you worry constantly about what you're going to say to others, you will have rehashed the conversation many times in your mind beforehand; this rehashing causes you to become more rigid and less adaptive during the conversation itself. The spontaneity and freedom of expression is missing from actual dialogues. Instead, you are like an actor reciting memorized lines. More important, you will communicate that you aren't listening with real intent. You will feel distracted and less than present.

As a high-need-for-achievement type, you're likely the type of person who replays conversations in your head. You analyze what you said, what you should have said, and what you might say in the future. These internal monologues, in which you reprimand yourself for a conversation that didn't go well, hurt your external dialogues. Your conversations are less rewarding and less productive than they should be because you're so worried before and after you have them. This is especially true if it's a difficult conversation—you have to deliver a negative performance review, explain a service problem to a customer, and so on.

When I ask leaders in groups why they struggle with these types of conversations, they make two points. First, they explain that they can't ensure the outcome of these talks. There is no telling how the other person may react, no matter how much they might have rehearsed their part of the conversation. They anticipate the other person reacting emotionally or with invective. They fear that what they are advocating or proposing will be shot down. Second, the time leading up to the tough conversation is more trying and more stressful than having the conversation itself. Jeffrey Kerr, a noted family therapist and executive coach, has found that the obsessing before the conversation causes conversation initiators to prepare in the wrong ways. Typically, this individual focuses on the content of the message rather than on the process or affect or how to communicate more effectively.

Kerr reflected on the typical patterns he observes in leaders who attempt to have tough conversations with their employees:

> Because of the worry, the leader, who is nervous already, begins the conversation by speaking. The tone of the speech is tense and very rational. And the longer the leader speaks the louder they speak, the faster they speak, and the more they speak. And this sets up the perfect scenario for failure. It sets off a vicious cycle. The person receiving the feedback begins to back away, listen less, and become defensive. The receiver immediately accesses his feelings and emotions and begins to feel embarrassed, exposed, humiliated, and shamed. The leader is a talking head who talks even more when he sees that the receiver's eyes have glazed over. By this time the interaction is beginning to go into a death spiral. And the leader continues to talk, and the listener quits listening and begins to figure out a way to get out of the room. And so it goes.[1]

One worry often leads to another worry. The dialogue doesn't go well, the frustrated manager starts ranting and raving, the direct report clearly isn't getting the message, and both leave the conversation feeling worse than they did before they began the interaction. The manager laments, "Why didn't person X listen more? Why didn't person X respond the way I wanted him to respond? Doesn't he understand that I'm giving him this feedback to help him? It's for his own good."

This last point goes to the source of worry. Contrary to what some people believe, it doesn't emanate only from the head, but can come from the heart as well. The manager in the previous paragraph cares about his direct report; he is giving him feedback that he believes will help his performance and his career. He is willing to have a tough conversation and deal with the situation because he's genuinely concerned about this individual. The more we care, the more we worry, and though we have the best of intentions, our intense anxiety can cause us to approach a person or a problem in the wrong way. Worry clouds our judgment, and we end up making bad decisions because of it.

I experienced this caring-inspired worry not only in my professional life but in my personal one. My daughter Sara was heading off to college for the first time. About three days before we all left to drop her off at school I realized how many things I hadn't taught her that I was sure she needed to know. I hadn't taught her how to invest her money. I hadn't taught her how to change a tire on a car. I hadn't taught her how to scrub a floor. I hadn't taught her how to connect her computer. I worried about how I had failed to teach Sara these critical life skills (or at least they seemed critical in my mind). So I sat her down to teach her all she needed to know. I talked more and more, and she listened less and less. She was polite, but tuned out. I warned her at one point that she should listen more carefully. I observed her gazing at her watch, anxious about her impending departure. Basically, I was clueless to her needs and obsessed with my agenda, with my own worries. I was doing neither myself nor her any good by fretting. All I really was doing was surfacing my worries but not digging down to figure out why I was so worried—and without doing that spadework, I was less effective as a father than I should have been.

From Worry to Guilt

You've probably heard people complain, "The more I have to do, the less I get done." If you're the type of ambitious professional who bites

off more than you can chew, you've probably experienced this feeling. You have so many tasks on your to-do list that you start worrying
incessantly about getting them done, and the more time you spend
worrying, the less energy you have for the tasks themselves.

Most of the time, high-need-for-achievement professionals feel fulfilled only when they have too many items on their agendas. At the same
time, they are always worrying that they won't cross off enough items
on their lists to experience relief and be successful. They believe they
will be less than adequate if they aren't balancing many projects. Jack
Gabarro once said, "When these high achievers have too many things
to do, they feel ongoing guilt, because no matter what they are accomplishing, they think they should be doing something else. They believe
they don't have enough time to accomplish everything and too many
things to do. If they are with a client, they think they should be back at
the office. If they are with family, they think they should be answering
e-mails. If they are getting ready to go to bed, they think they should
stay up an extra hour and get a jump start on the next day's work. When
they are enjoying positive feedback and reaching or exceeding their
goals, they worry that they're working so hard they'll burn out."

Highly ambitious, hard-charging professionals fan the flames of
their worry because of role overload or inter-role conflict.[2] Because
they have too much to do, they must sacrifice one thing for another
and in so doing set up the perfect scenario to worry even more because they are leaving some items behind. One friend lamented, "I
really do feel like I'm on a hamster wheel. I really do feel like I might
never step off. I worry whether I will ever get off and at the same time
worry what would happen if I did get off and couldn't step back on.
Either way I'm a mess. Either way I worry myself to sleep at night and
get up most mornings tired. What's pathetic about this pattern is that
I don't feel like I'm fully engaged in life unless I am worrying and tired
all the time."

Many highly successful people complain about being worn out most of the time. It just becomes a way of life. In fact, some high-need-for-achievement individuals worry so much they push their concerns from the realm of the real to that of the unlikely catastrophe.

Joanna, for instance, had attended an executive program at Harvard Business School when she said,

> Tom, as much as I liked the program in Boston, I left more worried than I had been before I arrived. Admittedly, I did get some answers, but I think I wrote down more questions with my newfound knowledge. All I've done since I arrived home is ruminate and worry about where I should begin and what the sequencing should be and who I should involve in the process. I worry about the plateaued partners in the firm who are not producing. I worry about the associates who are not being mentored and feel disconnected from the firm. I worry about the lack of women partners and associates. I thought we had dealt with this issue but it seems as prevalent today as it was ten years ago. All I know is that the more I think about these issues the more I realize that I can't do it alone.

The longer Joanna worried, the more she lost context and perspective. It was as if she were making up problems, or at the very least magnifying them beyond their actual size. She was beginning to see everything as catastrophic. She knew she needed help and was basically stuck in the mud, spinning her wheels. Everything seemed urgent and important. She couldn't differentiate between what needed to be done today or in three weeks or three years. She didn't know who she should seek help from. Rather than delegate or outsource or request assistance from colleagues and bosses, she kept all this agonizing internal until she spoke with me. Logically, Joanna could have

moderated or even eliminated some of her worries by gathering resources or proposing a new program. But the worrying trap discourages action—especially new and innovative action—in favor of passive
fretting. People who spend all their time worrying lack the energy and
initiative necessary to change. They find it difficult to make the leap
from the quadrant of doing the right thing poorly to the quadrant of
the doing the right thing well. They become so consumed by what they
don't know and the mistakes they're making that they can't gather
themselves and gain necessary knowledge and learn from their mistakes. They are too worried to have the courage to take on the projects
and the fresh learning that will enable them to do the right thing well.

Do You Love Me as Much as I Love You?

Contrary to the stereotype, most hard-charging, ambitious professionals care what others think about them. In fact, they care deeply. When
they enter the office in the morning, they may put on their corporate
face and seem like they're all about business, but underneath they're
vitally concerned with how their colleagues see them. For this reason,
much of the worry that transpires in the workplace relates to how they
perceive their relationships with others.

Consider the types of worries that typically beset the driven
professional:

- We worry if the boss likes us as much as she does our corporate competition.

- We worry that our subordinates like us and respect us less
  than someone else in the organization.

- We worry that the CEO or other top executives don't know
  who we are or don't recognize our contribution.

- We worry when a colleague quits initiating conversations with us and seems to distance himself from us.

- We worry that we have let down a valued customer or client.

- We worry that a supplier feels as if we have betrayed his trust.

The worry is endless when it comes to relationships, not only in our professional but in our private lives. We don't think about it or direct the worry consciously, but it's integral to the human condition—and being a high-need-for-achievement professional exacerbates it.

Think about worry as a type of social exchange. Most high-need-for-achievement personalities start agonizing when it seems like an unequal exchange is occurring: for instance, Bill appears to be far less interested in your business relationship than you are; he doesn't call or e-mail you as much as you call and e-mail him. Some business pundits have referred to this phenomenon as *the power of least interest*. In other words, the person in a relationship who has the least interest in the relationship has the most power in the relationship. If I have less interest in becoming acquainted with you than you have in getting to know me, then I have the power in the relationship. People worry all the time about these power inequities in work relationships, and that's when problems result—problems that harm careers and hurt organizations.[3]

It doesn't take much of a shift to a least-interest relationship dynamic to catalyze worry. A boss may seem to depend on you less for certain tasks than he used to. You realize that you've asked a colleague to join you for lunch three times in the past month and he hasn't reciprocated with his own invitation. When a customer fails to return your phone calls with his usual speed, and when you do talk to him, he seems distant. You start asking yourself questions: "Does this person care as much about me as I care about him? Does the other person want to put forth the time and energy to enhance this relationship?

Does the other person give any cues or signals that he wants to invest in the relationship?"

When I mention the power of least interest in seminars, the first thing that comes to mind for most participants is a personal relationship. Most think of a time that they wanted the attention of someone else and weren't getting it. They reflect upon the actions they took to change the power dynamics in the relationship. They try and figure out whether it was even worth it to invest in the effort. They worry if they want to terminate a relationship with someone else, how the other person will react.

We are constantly gauging the symmetry we have with others in one-to-one relationships in groups and in organizations as well. Frustration, fear, and anxiety all play into the particular drama that unfolds. We strive for equal partnerships in all our relationships. Even though a manager may have a formal position that places him higher in the hierarchy, we still want to know that the other person is as invested in the relationship as much as we are. This desire will never change. And the worry will never abate. Notice how many dysfunctional actions take place in organizations and in families when an individual within those systems feels underappreciated, excluded, threatened, or inadequate. When people believe that they have received a signal that they don't matter, they often respond with dysfunctional behavior.

Lois had worked for Jenny for three years in a consulting firm. Though they weren't exactly friends, they always got along well and enjoyed an effective work relationship. Unbeknownst to Lois, Jenny had both personal and professional problems. She was going through a divorce and custody battle, and she was under pressure from her boss to improve her group's results. Jenny was the type of boss who internalized most of her problems. Though she was friendly and communicative, she made a consistent effort not to let her pain show—she didn't burden her friends with tales of her marital woes or her work colleagues with stories about how management was leaning hard on her to increase results because the firm had lost a major client (not in Jenny's group) and was asking all group leaders to do better.

At first, Lois noticed that Jenny was a bit more distant in their conversations—she tended to end them abruptly and adopted a perfunctory manner when it came to their casual talk about nonwork matters. Then she went to a major industry workshop and didn't invite Lois to join her—Lois had gone with her to the previous two conferences (Lois didn't know that Jenny's budget had been cut and she couldn't afford to bring anyone). Finally, when Lois approached Jenny and asked to talk about a problem she was having with another member of her group, Jenny brushed her off, saying that she'd have to resolve it on her own and that she was pressed for time that day.

Feeling devalued, Lois started talking negatively about Jenny behind her back to other colleagues. She complained about Jenny's coldness and unhelpful attitude. She became convinced not only that had she fallen out of favor, but that Jenny planned to fire her. Desperate, Lois went behind Jenny's back and arranged a meeting with Jenny's boss, telling him she believed that Jenny was no longer an effective manager and was creating a poor work environment through her demeanor. She requested a transfer to another group.

Lois worried so much that the balance of power in the relationship had shifted that she was acting dysfunctionally—or at least, she was acting in a way that wasn't in her or Jenny's best interest. Rather than communicate to Jenny the seriousness of her concerns and the need to address them, she chose another route that wasn't good for her career or for the group.

Be Ambiguous at Your Peril

You may recall a story I related earlier about how I had just finished teaching a class on motivation and was leaving the class when a student stopped me and complimented me on how great the discussion was and how, because I was in a hurry and distracted by other matters, I just stared at him blankly and moved on.

If I were this student, I'd be thinking to myself, "I wonder if Tom didn't hear me." Or, "What an arrogant jerk. He's always talking about listening and being authentic and he just blew me off." Or perhaps the thinking would progress to, "Well, I made a comment in class today. I wonder if it wasn't that good." Or, "I thought I was doing well in De-Long's class. Maybe I'm not." If I had simply spent two seconds to acknowledge this student's compliment, I could have stopped him from engaging in this counterproductive thinking.

We have a tendency to interpret any message, behavior, or even a lack of information ambiguously; in turn, all ambiguous behavior is interpreted negatively. If the leader of a company shares a confusing strategy with future employees, the employees will worry that the organization's direction is not well thought out. If a manager sends an ambiguous e-mail about a particular client, the receiver will think something is wrong not only with the client but with the relationship between the manager and client. In my situation with the student, my behavior was ambiguous. It allowed him to create a negative interpretation of my ambiguous behavior. This was not the way to create a connected and secure relationship.

Consider how you respond to ambiguity at work. If you're like most people, you probably never realized how much ambiguity surrounds you or how it causes you to worry. Your boss doesn't tell you, "Good job" after reviewing your analysis, and you wonder if he's thinking, "Lousy job." It seems logical to ask him why he didn't tell you good job, but logic has nothing to do with it. As a driven professional, you dread the possibility that he thinks your work is bad; better to leave it ambiguous than to know the brutal truth, or so your reasoning goes.

To counteract the worrying that is exacerbated by ambiguity, here are some tactics that can help:

- Force yourself to question the individual involved to determine what he or she really means: Yes, I know all your high-need-for-achievement instincts are telling you not to, but no matter how bad the truth might be, it's better than the alternative. If you need further motivation, remind yourself that passivity is the coward's way out.

- Make a real or mental note of all positive responses when you confront people about their ambiguous statements: Most of the time, forcing definitive responses from ambiguous speakers will reassure you—you'll discover their ambiguity was inadvertent and not meant to demean you. Keeping this fact in mind will help you worry less the next time someone speaks ambiguously.

- Do something when your worst fears are realized: Let's say it's true; your boss really does believe you're not working up to your potential. If this is the case, don't stew and fret and complain to friends and family. Instead, take action:

  1. Get specifics about what you're doing wrong, what more you should be doing, and so forth.

  2. Create a plan to correct the problem.

  3. Charge someone with making sure you carry out the plan.

  High-need-for-achievement professionals are doers, and if you remain passive, you'll simply worry more.

- Finally, never forget that while some worry is normal, excessive worry festers and withers the soul: It is the prelude to cynicism and negativity. While worry might motivate us short term, at the end of the day it can become the defining way we live.

Fortunately, worry can be managed, and the first step to managing it and the three other traps I've discussed is *awareness*. Making yourself conscious of these traps is a great first step to avoid falling into them. Next, try some of the tactics I've suggested here; they can help you escape the worrying traps you might fall into. Perhaps most important is creating a larger strategy for change and improvement to overcome the anxieties that make us rigid, fearful, and helpless. This strategy is the subject of the following chapters.

PART IV

GETTING
OVER IT

Tools for Turning
Fear of Change into
Fuel for Success

CHAPTER TEN

Put It Behind You

Now that we're aware of the traps that can keep us from changing, growing, and succeeding, what can we do about them? As it turns out, there's a lot that can be done, but I'd like to demonstrate the prescriptive possibilities by way of Jeff Gardner, a character I created for an earlier book on leadership.[1] Jeff was the highly successful partner of a small consulting firm, and I ended the story in that book with him reflecting on all the tasks that confronted him as he prepared to land in Boston after a long transcontinental flight. Now let's continue the story.

At the end of the flight Jeff felt that all his ruminations about his many pressures and responsibilities had left him more tired than rested. The complaints of younger associates and vice presidents he managed still echoed in his head. He couldn't escape his frustrations about carrying one partner who hated travel, didn't know how to sell business, and—while good at producing work that was assigned to him—hadn't progressed as the firm had grown.

There was also the problem of clients who were becoming more demanding as their financial woes mounted. They seemed to be more aggressive in their demands for not only lower rates but more attention for less money. They also seemed much more willing to challenge everything Jeff suggested to them.

There was also his wife, Marie, and their two girls. Marie had less patience and was more outspoken about the perceived promises that Jeff had broken than she had in the past. She had told him just before he left on his trip, "Jeff, in our fifteen years of marriage I don't know of a time when you've had to choose between work and family that you've chosen family." Jeff found himself feeling more and more guilty when she made these types of observations. She was stating her position more stridently than she had on other occasions; her patience was wearing thin.

What Saved Jeff Gardner

Shortly after returning from his trip, Jeff met with the firm's managing partner, who asked him, "Jeff, do you want to rise higher in the organization and perhaps someday run the firm? Before you tell me what you think I want to hear, I want you to take some time over the next month and ask yourself some tough questions about your career. More important, I want you to ask yourself some questions about yourself. If you want to move up in the firm and take on more responsibility, I think you have a long a way to go. It will take some real change on your part. So think about it. Think seriously about it. The answer isn't obvious. Come back in a month and let's talk again."

After a couple of weekends walking on the beach on Long Island with Marie and having heart-to-heart discussions about matters personal and professional, Jeff decided he needed to deal with his fears and frustrations. Marie noted later that the talks she shared with Jeff on the beach were the first conversations in ten years in which he had opened up about these deeper issues. When they talked these days, they would generally have maintenance conversations, focusing on who would pick up the clothes at the laundry or the kids from school. Everything was about logistics. Now, they were talking in a way Marie remembered from when they were younger, when Jeff was genuine in his expression of feelings and no topic was out of bounds.

Jeff had spent a professional lifetime managing image, never showing any signs of weakness. Jeff thought that any sign of vulnerability might have a negative impact. Along the career journey, Jeff had learned early on that he needed to maneuver carefully around anything that might lead to an "emotional incident" at work, anything that meant he might be embarrassed because he didn't know something or might appear *soft*—that is, too concerned about his people and not concerned enough about results. You cut that part out of you if you wanted to succeed moving up the firm. At least that is what Gardner had believed since he was an associate.

When Jeff reported back to the managing partner a month later and told him that he was interested in more responsibility, his mentor pushed back and asked if he was serious. Jeff replied, "I really would like to work on the human dimension of leading and managing but to be perfectly honest, I don't know how and whether I can really get there. I want to and I know that I should know by now how to get there."

"I'm not sure I can do it" was a critical admission. It meant that Jeff had begun to acknowledge that he didn't have all the answers. The self-reflection evident in this statement meant that Jeff had acknowledged to himself his own fallibility and limitations and that an opportunity to learn existed. From an interpersonal standpoint, it conveyed that he had the courage to show vulnerability, that he had gone through some internal process in which he had begun to think through what had gone wrong and why. This one line was what the managing partner had been waiting and hoping for.

What many command-and-control leaders fail to grasp is that admissions of fallibility, uncertainty, and doubt are actually signs of strength. These admissions propel individuals from doing the wrong thing well to doing the right thing poorly. It's what gives them the impetus to learn, to change, and to grow. Before continuing with Jeff's story, I'd like you to pause and engage in the same sort of reflection that Jeff did. The following are questions that high-need-for-achievement professionals don't often ask themselves. They raise the possibility that you may have spent less time than you should have actually slowing down and acknowledging that you may not have all the answers. I realize that most hard-driving managers and executives have been socialized to believe they cannot admit vulnerability to themselves or others. I would urge you to get past this misconception and realize that such admissions will enhance your productivity and career. So, consider:

- Do you regret any significant decisions you've made about your career? If you had to do it over again, would you do it differently?

- Have there been times when you treated your people unfairly? When you failed to listen and learn and instead directed and dictated?

- Do you feel you've been working at peak capacity in recent years? If not, why not?

- Are you unwilling to admit your mistakes to your direct reports? To your bosses? To your colleagues?

- Have you asked anyone for help recently? Have you admitted you didn't know something and needed to learn it? Have you asked for coaching?

- If you were to be completely honest with your boss and knew that there would be no negative repercussions, what secret fear or anxiety would you admit to him?

- Do you believe that you're in the right job, in the right group, and in the right organization? Or do you feel there's a mismatch between where you are now and what you want to accomplish?

The Mentor Who Actually Mentored

The managing partner of Jeff's firm had a friend, Charles, who was a professor at a business school and whom he trusted to tell the whole truth all the time. It didn't mean full disclosure of anything and everything, but it did mean that Charles could be relied on to be transparent and blunt if necessary to make the point. The managing partner requested that Charles work with Jeff. The first time they met, Charles set the ground rules for their relationship, the most important one being the simple instruction, "Put the past in the past." Charles didn't want Jeff obsessing about paths not taken, mistakes made, and opportunities missed. Instead, he wanted him to face the truth about his past and learn to let go of it.

Charles wanted Jeff to own up to his mistakes, apologize where necessary, and move on. But the most difficult challenge facing Jeff was acknowledging that after all these years he had been less effective than he could have been. He realized that there were many colleagues and employees in his career journey who had been derailed through his blind ambition. It was as though his past had opened up into a view of colleagues to whom he could have provided more support. He was realizing too late that many professionals had quit the firm or had asked to be transferred to other departments at least in part because of his behaviors. Jeff needed to acknowledge and get past the fact that many people had paid a price for his success, and this was difficult for him.

Charles also taught Jeff how to create a unique type of agenda that guided behavior and new skill development rather than showed a list of easily ignored line items. Creating this agenda refined Jeff's purpose and direction, guiding him through the fog of everyday pressures. Charles told Jeff of research demonstrating that managers who had specific items to achieve in a particular time frame were far more successful than those who simply worked off a to-do list. Through an iterative process, Charles and Jeff created such an agenda, and Charles had Gardner place copies everywhere: the bathroom mirror, in a picture frame on the desk next to the picture of Marie, in the car. And Charles called Jeff every other day at the beginning of the process to make sure Jeff was focused and not distracted. And slowly, over time, Jeff made progress using a focused approach.

How Embarrassing Can It Be?

Jeff later reported that, while the agenda was critical for him in making progress, what helped him just as much was the admonition to put the past in the past. How trite. How simple. How effective! Jeff had assumed that because he was successful with clients he could cover up any deficiencies. He also assumed that he had solidified basic habits over time, and they were now part of his DNA. He never really reflected on how and why he acted the way he did—why he was unable to have completely open and honest conversations with his wife and with his colleagues. Putting the past in the past became a kind of mantra for Jeff; it reminded him to differentiate between his past reality and the story he told himself about this past. Charles pointed out, "It is not what actually happened in your past that is important but what you told yourself about yourself that mattered. It has to do with the story you created about the past."

Too often, these stories revolve around long-simmering resentments and even vengeful feelings. Some successful managers can't get past how their first boss denied them a promotion when "I deserved it." Some fume silently about how they should have taken a job a headhunter offered but were "seduced" into staying with lesser jobs by smooth-talking bosses. Others obsess about promises the organization made to them that were never kept.

Most of the high-need-for-achievement people in organizations rarely surface these stories. They cling to the bitter memories rather than articulate them and let them go. Speaking the truth about these experiences, no matter how painful, is a highly productive exercise as long as people do so with a close friend or therapist. Once the regret or anger is verbalized, it ceases to have such a strong hold. They find it easier to let it go, and instead of directing their time and energy to replaying these thoughts in their minds, they can use this time and energy more productively.

Try the following exercise to put your past in the past:

1. Identify the story you tell yourself about why you haven't achieved everything you wanted to achieve. When you think about why you were passed over for a promotion or why your career at a great company sidetracked, what is the story you repeat to yourself? Repetition is a key for identifying this story; you've told it to yourself more than once and probably multiple times over the years.

2. Now determine the primary emotion you feel when you tell this story. Is it anger, sadness, frustration, shame? Focus on the specific event or situation that caused you to feel this emotion. What about this event or situation has such a powerful

effect? Try to identify specific things you said or did and/or that others said or did.

3. Find a trusted confidant—a boss, mentor, coach, spouse, or close friend—and verbalize both the story and the powerful feeling. Be completely honest and open in doing this step.

4. The next time you find yourself surfacing this story, repeat to yourself, "Put the past in the past."

This exercise will need to be done more than once. In other words, you may need to have more than one discussion with a trusted confidant about what happened, and you may want to repeat the mantra "Put the past in the past" more than once. But it's worth the effort, because after you're able to confront the story and the emotion attached to it and recognize that it belongs in the past rather than the present, you'll enjoy much greater freedom in your work behavior. You'll be much more likely to take on a challenging assignment or make the effort to learn a new skill.

A close friend reminded me just a few months ago of an exercise he witnessed that helped people get distance from these past experiences. When my friend was an independent consultant before he became head of human resources at a large technology company, he taught in a number of leadership development programs. During those years we both worked with an expert in team building named Horst Abraham. Abraham would take groups through various exercises and discuss what had happened during the process. I also was privy to what team members would discuss as Abraham facilitated the interaction within the group.

At the end of the session Abraham would ask these professionals to put their arms in the air and move them from front to back high behind their heads. They were to repeat after him, "Put it behind you" at least three times. Every participant would follow his instructions and do exactly as he had said—all took it very seriously. My friend and I often watched this exercise, and we were impressed and amazed that Abraham could get these professionals to do something so basic. We would shake our heads in disbelief that a facilitator could actually do this without smiling—that he could take it so seriously and have others share that serious attitude.

As my colleague and I talked about these experiences, I began thinking about what had occurred in my past that I had difficulty letting go of, and my main memory was of the way I had been treated by a group of faculty earlier in my career. I felt that they had voted me off their island because of some of the career decisions I had made after leaving graduate school. Every time I ran into one of these professors, I would begin to have a visceral reaction. I was angry and also embarrassed at the same time. I was sure they were looking down on me in judgment. I was sure they were thinking that I had thrown my education away by joining an inferior college at an inferior school. I was sure they were thinking and feeling all of these things. Why I was sure I don't know. But I had created enough stories in my head to support this belief; I had manufactured plenty of signs from these professors' words and deeds to reinforce my certainty that I was being shunned. They never invited me to attend conferences and present papers. They always passed me over for some award in favor of someone who was in "the club." Funny thing was—I had thought I was in the club while I was there, but for some reason they had decided that I wasn't worthy or successful enough. Or so I thought.

My friend really taught me something, though, when he shared a story about a time he arrived at home from work feeling grumpy and irritated. He reported that he went on and on at the dinner table with his four kids and wife listening—not responding, just listening. Out of the blue, his youngest daughter Meredith said, "Dad, you need to put it behind you." She said in a soft-spoken, understated way. But my friend heard it and did a double take. He looked at Meredith once, then again, and then began to smile. He had been caught. All the kids began to smile and they began to make the motion Abraham had taught him; he had used the simple tactic as an intervention years earlier when the kids were fighting with one another.

Once my friend told the story, nothing more needed to be said. I looked at him and his wife—and we all laughed.

Not Letting Go

Over the years I've witnessed myriad professionals blame other professionals when their careers weren't flourishing, or obsess about how some other person prevented them from achieving a goal or fulfilling their potential. I have a good friend who has expressed frustration on numerous occasions that his father didn't support him professionally. He has recounted the same incidents over the years with great passion, and his message revolves around the following: "Dad didn't loan me the money I needed to buy two different businesses. If only he had trusted me, I would have had a much more rewarding and fulfilling career."

I point out to my friend that holding on to these feelings is debilitating from a career standpoint; that this long-ago slight has such a hold on him that it prevents him from savoring what he has accomplished and from trusting himself (as he feels his father refused to do). He is reluctant to tackle a new project or take any type of risk because he hears his father's voice of distrust in his head. And so he doesn't change and grow. Letting go of cognitive and affective impact of this memory is the only way to be more satisfied in the future. It is the only way to be vulnerable again, to have the courage to try something new, to experience doing the right thing poorly in order to be able to do the right thing well.

You Don't Have the Whole Story

Morgan Stanley's John Mack also provided me with a lesson that I've found facilitates the process of letting go in driven, ambitious professionals. After we had worked closely together for seven years, he taught me the value of listening deeply, listening between the lines. I observed on a number of occasions how he listened to an investment banker who had the most convincing story about a particular situation. I would listen and buy into the banker's story—it seemed absolutely credible. Shortly after meeting with the banker, John would call in someone who had a different perspective on the same story. I would listen and, to my surprise, I would find this version of events just as credible as the earlier one, even though there were significant differences between the two. I was completely confused.

When we were by ourselves, Mack would turn to me and, with a wry smile, explain, "You see Tom, there are always two sides to every story." We'd talk through the situation and he would tell me what he had heard—what he thought was the path between the two stories that mirrored the possible truth. I learned that as much as I want to believe one person's story, there will be someone with another perspective that is just as convincing.

When you view your own world and your own behavior from a narrow perspective (which most driven professionals do), then you're essentially stuck in your routines and standard way of operating. Other people (like a boss or a coach) may try to tell you that you need to change—or a voice inside your head may encourage you to try something new—but as long as you continue to see things as you always have, you will remain stuck where you are. Putting it behind you enlarges your perspective. You are no longer bound by your fears and resentments but can open your mind to other possibilities. When you grasp that multiple realities exist based on your history, your current context and your goals, you free yourself to pursue these realities.

That brings us to another exercise:

Write your story from another perspective. Go back to the earlier exercise and then write it as if you were another person who was involved in your story (usually the antagonist). For instance, let's say the story you obsess about is how you trusted a customer who promised to provide your company with continued business but who then suddenly switched his account to a competitor. The story you've been telling yourself is that he was a liar and a jerk; that he made a fool of you because you had told your boss that the account was fine; and that you felt naive for being so trusting.

In this instance, then, your goal would be to write the story from your customer's perspective—what went through his mind as he turned his back on your company and decided to go to a competitor.

You don't necessarily have to believe the alternative story you tell, but you should try to imagine a credible version of events from the other person's perspective. The point is to recognize that your version is not the only possible version, and this recognition will loosen its grip on you and allow you to let it go.

In short, understanding that there are two (or more) sides to every story gets us prepared to change. When we realize that the single story we've been telling ourselves can be limiting, we start thinking of other possible interpretations. We get in the mood to move forward and create a network of support. We begin to look for a particular person who will take us by the hand and care for us more than we care for ourselves. That is the next step in the process of getting unstuck and moving on to where we want to go.

CHAPTER ELEVEN

Second Captain First Choose

YOU MAY HAVE NOTICED THAT IN CHAPTER 10 I placed special emphasis on a number of people: friends; Charles, who coached the fictional Jeff Gardner; and Morgan Stanley's John Mack. This emphasis was deliberate. We cannot escape the traps that snare us unless we have people who can help us find a way out. It is our network of support that allows us to muster the courage to confront our anxieties and be sufficiently open and honest.

The problem, of course, is that high-need-for-achievement professionals create an external portrayal of rugged individualists, being completely self-sufficient. Because of a variety of factors—the socialization process, the model created by leaders who came before them, the cultures of the companies that they came up through—they believe that they should be John Wayne rather than Alan Alda. They think they need to be tough and independent, that they can't ask anyone for help if they're struggling. I know more than one troubled executive who believes that others will think he is "soft" if he admits uncertainty.

Consequently, many ambitious, hard-charging individuals fail to create a strong network of people who can help them when they require help. They try to go it alone, not realizing that this strategy will send them deeper into their respective traps. While they might have a few colleagues they're friends with and in whom they confide, these people often are not the right choice for their support network. In most instances, driven professionals confide in people who tell them what they *want* to hear, not what they *need* to hear.

It's natural to choose people who share your beliefs and values for your team; it's natural to select as confidants individuals who will make you feel good about yourself. The problem, of course, is that these individuals won't challenge you to change. To help you choose your team of advisers properly, let me tell you about how we chose baseball teams when I was growing up in Portland.

Making Tough Choices for Your Team

Growing up, I spent months on the playgrounds and in the streets playing every sport under the sun. When we played baseball on 23rd and Stephens Street in Portland, we took the game so seriously that we would slide on the pavement if the play was going to be close. We started each game by choosing captains. One captain would call out, "Second Captain First Choose" and another kid would shout, "First Captain Second Choose." The second captain was able to choose the first person for his team and the second captain got to choose who got up to the plate first. Obviously, the second captain would choose the best person, and then the first captain would choose the next-best person, and so on, until the worst people were chosen at the end. As I think about the process we used to select teams, I cringe at our insensitivity. Still, we were also focused on a goal: winning. We knew that the people we picked for our teams determined whether we would win or lose, and we were absolutely ruthless in our choices. We would bypass our best friends for people we didn't like who could hit with power. If we needed a pitcher, we'd pass over a friend who couldn't throw well in favor of an acquaintance with a wicked curve.

My point is that we knew how to assemble a team with a clear goal in mind. I'm suggesting that if you want to change and grow as a person and as a professional, you'll use the same pragmatic approach to assembling your support network.

The first part of this chapter will focus on how and why to choose the people who will tell you the truth in a supportive way; it will also look at how to find a partner, mentor, or guide who cares as much or more about you than you do about yourself. The second part of the chapter will discuss the importance of the truth you receive from your team and how to use it.

Soloing Is for the Fearful

No one can do it alone. No one. Try it and see where you end up. All the data on change emphasizes the importance of having a hand to hold. In Gene Dalton's seminal work on the common dominators for change, the first dimension is feeling that change is necessary.[1] This is what Jeff Gardner experienced when the managing partner of the firm gave him the opportunity to see that change was an imperative for development on many levels. Dalton's second dimension for change to happen is the need for a "respected other" in the process. Call it what you want—coach, friend, managing partner, mentor, spouse, partner, therapist—but someone must be there to help you through the rough patches. This means identifying and recruiting this respected other who cares more about you than you care about you, and it means creating a team that will support you where you want to go.

In many organizations today, however, people lack a natural process for finding a mentor or confidant; you can't expect to be automatically "given" this support, even if you're deemed a high-potential.

The following story illustrates how companies have subordinated this support process.

During leadership development seminars or in other forums in which I'm acting as a facilitator, I ask participants to write down the name of a person that they have viewed as a leader, mentor, or teacher. The only criterion is that this individual must be someone with whom they have had a relationship (as opposed to the leader of a country or a business superstar). In most instances, older participants have an easier time with this assignment than younger ones; they often ask, "Can I write down more than one?" The younger participants, on the other hand, ask for more time.

Older professionals are more likely to have deep, personal relationships with mentors and leaders because as they were rising through the ranks, organizations were smaller and more intimate. They felt more like families. Senior professionals in the organization were expected to treat a new hire like a daughter or son. They were responsible for helping their people succeed. I don't mean responsible in some vague sense of the term; management expected veteran professionals to take charge of their direct reports and to do what was necessary to help them perform well.

Mentoring and teaching were key skills for bosses, and when their people did well, bosses were esteemed for their ability to develop younger associates. These skills weren't part of a formal professional assessment or performance evaluation processes. Instead, there was an implicit understanding that the senior person would watch out for his people and guide them as needed so that they would succeed in the organization. Their people rarely would leave because it would be like leaving family; they would be disappointing a father or mother figure.

Having this mentor kept high-need-for-achievement individuals from falling into anxiety-ridden traps. They always had someone to talk to if they ran into problems or were feeling fearful. They always

had someone who could offer advice that was heartfelt and, more often than not, right on the money. More to the point, these protegés
had someone who could impress upon them the necessity of change
and who they respected when the mentor challenged them for being
complacent or for stubbornly trying to do the wrong thing well.

As you can imagine, without such guides, people can stumble into
traps and fail to embrace change. It might seem that clinging to routines and refusing to try something new is a strategy that will keep
them safe, but in fact it keeps them from growing. A wise mentor would
tell them that; but today, these mentors are difficult to find.

If you're a high-need-for-achievement professional working in just
about any type of organization today, you likely lack the support that
someone in your position enjoyed in the past. If you're older—say,
over forty—the people you used to turn to for help have either retired
or been fired; and if they're still around, they no longer have the time
or the incentive from management to provide this support.

If you're under forty, you probably know the formal process of
mentoring has deteriorated. Many young professionals use the term
free agent to describe their lack of connection with their bosses and
their organizations; they often feel this way from their very first day on
the job. They define work as completing a contract rather than committing to a larger collective.

This feeling is no doubt justified. It's not that senior professionals
aren't interested in mentoring but that the increased demands of their
jobs rob them of the time and energy to do so. Veteran managers are
under great pressure to sell and cross-sell business, to be involved in
myriad organizational duties, and to continue to do excellent work with
current clients or customers. If they are asked to mentor others, it's usually not one or two people but five or ten. Feeling overwhelmed, they go
through the motions of mentoring. They hold superficial lunches once a
quarter and push the meal along in order to get back to their real work.

Even worse, they inadvertently communicate to those they mentor that the task of guiding them is a burden rather than an opportunity.

When It Works, It's Magic

Imagine going through your life without a close friend, a parent, an older sibling. In other words, imagine that you lack someone you trust and respect, who can give you advice, who can impart wisdom. Imagine hitting all of life's rough spots—a divorce, illness, etc.—without someone who's been there and done that. Without these individuals to talk and listen to, we'd be lost. More to the point, we'd fall into various life traps—we'd marry the same type of person we married earlier; we'd use drinking or drugs to escape a negative situation; we'd zone out in front of the television and fail to spend our time in meaningful pursuits.

The same behavior happens to people in work situations when they lack a trusted "elder" or more experienced colleague who is invested in their success. They need guides who can listen objectively, who will level with them, who can offer the benefit of their experience. Consider how valuable such individuals are to driven professionals by way of the following two examples.

Sheila, a managing partner of a leading law firm, reflected on how her mentor helped her earlier in her career:

> John reached out to me when I had hit a rough patch and
> told me that someday I could lead the firm. He told me that
> he had more confidence in me than I had in myself. This
> one conversation in the earlier stages of my career was like
> a meteor for me. I felt like I had been shot through the roof
> with adrenaline. That conversation stays with me today now
> that I've led the firm for over ten years. And when John died,
> it was as traumatic for me as burying my two parents. I'm not

sure I'm over it now. John made me be a better lawyer. He showed me confidence in my darkest hours. How could I ever forget him?

Andrew was the president of a university, and Jason was beginning his career as an assistant professor at a competing institution in the same state. Jason had just finished postdoctoral work at MIT, and he was supporting his wife and his two little girls. Weeks before school was to begin in September, he began to have panic attacks. He would find himself wide-eyed and sure that he was going to die from his racing heart. He felt that the journey ahead was too steep, the expectations too great. And his body began to respond as it did.

Andrew reached out to this young professor and told him that he too had experienced great stress starting out. He took time out from his presidential duties to reach out. Andrew would call Jason out of the blue. He would invite him to school basketball games. He would invite him to hear special speakers who were on campus. Later in Jason's career, Andrew asked him to help with improving his senior team and thinking through an organizational restructuring. From the time Jason was twenty-nine until he was dean of a school, Andrew was there for personal and professional advice. He listened more than he talked. More important, Jason knew he was there.

There is a John or Andrew in your work life waiting to provide you with support, even though you may have to be more proactive in requesting help rather than have someone reach out to you, as Sheila and Jason experienced. We often believe that an executive isn't interested in mentoring us or a senior colleague is too busy and too important to bother having a heart-to-heart conversation. We assume that we can't talk honestly and openly to a top executive because we'll be seen as weak or overly emotional. In fact, many managers want to have direct reports and other employees seek their guidance. Even though they might not look or act like they want this role, the majority do. The main problem, of course, is time. Many bosses have so much on their plates that adding mentoring to the list feels like one responsibility too many. If you approach them at the wrong time and ask for advice, they may respond brusquely. The key, therefore, is recognizing when they seem more relaxed and have a break in their schedule; that's when they'll be open to the idea of mentoring. When people gain wisdom and experience after years of work, they usually want to share what they've learned; they want to help others on their way up. In fact, a defining moment sneaks up on most of us when we realize that we have developed or matured to a point where we care more about helping others develop than enhancing our own résumés.

Therefore, seek out someone who might provide help. Despite appearances, he or she will be honored by your request and will provide an empathetic ear as well as advice to make sure you stay out of the traps that catch most driven professionals unaware.

Choose a Team

Why did it take me until my oldest daughter was thirteen years old before I asked her for three things I could do to be a better father? Why did I wait all that time to hear what was on the mind of a very astute observer?

When I speak to leaders about the last time they solicited feedback from their children, they give me a blank look. They hadn't thought of actually sitting down and asking those close to them what they could do to improve. Or what should they be doing more of or less of. Most worry about what the feedback will be. They envision worst-case scenarios in which their loved ones list all their faults in excruciating detail. Those individuals who act on my suggestion, however, are surprised by what their children tell them. Younger children invariably say that they want their parents to be around more or to read more books or play with their trucks with them. This isn't impossible to achieve. Yet because of our fear of what we will hear, we don't ask. The same holds true for our significant others, friends, and siblings. We think we know what they think about us because we imagine it; we create our own version of how they see us and it becomes reality. Only it is usually quite a bit off from how they really view us. Only an honest conversation about this subject will reveal their true perceptions.

Don't allow your preconceived notions about other people's perceptions prevent you from recruiting a team of people to be your advisory board. Whether you draw from your professional circle or friends and family, overcome your fears of what they *might* say and focus on the value of what they actually *will* say.

Choose individuals at work who are kindred spirits. This doesn't mean select colleagues who think just like you do and will provide unconditional support no matter what you do. Kindred spirits are not "yes" men and women. Instead, you find their ideas and values in sync with your own, and you trust them to be honest with you. When you find these kindred spirits, choose one or two of them who observe you in your daily patterns. They should be individuals who possess the following traits:

- An ability to communicate clearly and honestly

- Empathy

- Perceptivity about what makes people tick

- A sense of shared values and purpose (they view work in a similar way to you)

The colleagues you select can be bosses, direct reports, or colleagues. Typically, people select individuals who are older and more experienced (and theoretically, wiser), but you may find that others in the organization provide you with the best feedback.

In terms of the process for requesting assistance and obtaining feedback from these individuals, here are some suggestions:

1. Approach the one or two people you've selected and ask them if they are willing to be your advisers: Explain that you hope they'll be available to talk to you honestly, provide feedback, and engage in conversations where they pull no punches. Suggest that you would appreciate if they would take on the hybrid role of coach/confidant.

2. Schedule regular meetings: These can take place once a week or once a month, but the key is to establish a schedule so that you meet regularly rather than sporadically (or not at all).

3. Figure out how you can structure the relationship so that the mentor gets something out of it as well: Don't shy away from reciprocity.

4. Force yourself to speak freely during these meetings: Unlike most conversations with colleagues, these dialogues should be brutally honest. You don't have to hide your feelings or try to put a positive spin on things. This strategy won't work unless you drop your mask and expose what you're thinking and feeling.

5. Demand that your advisers be equally honest: They may not want to hurt your feelings. They may worry that you'll be angry with them if they speak honestly. Therefore, you need to keep reiterating that you need them to speak the truth; that you will not hold what they say against them.

6. Reflect on these conversations: When you hear things in the moment, you may not be able to process them fully. Reserve time later—ideally, when you're alone and don't have anything

pressing to do—to think deeply about what you've been told. Reflection helps you absorb the full impact of the messages you've heard and consider what to do about them.

Broaden your network with "outside" people who possess the four traits listed earlier. Select your significant other (if you have one) but don't rely solely on this person as your confidant. Your partner can only act as therapist for so long. Choose a coach or counselor if you think you need someone who can point out places where you know you have blind spots but aren't sure where they are or what they are. Choose a couple of very good friends who are your friends for a reason—you trust them to give you a sense of the difference between the forest and the trees—to point out when you are calling white black and black white.

Most important, choose those individuals who you know won't tell you what you want to hear. High-need-for-achievement professionals, as we've discussed, have healthy egos and are sensitive to criticism. For this reason, you may find yourself stacking the deck in your favor by selecting people whom you know in your heart of hearts won't level with you. Though you may tell yourself they'll try to be honest, you recognize that they will be upbeat and complimentary most of the time and help you preserve your ego.

To that point, I'm reminded of an e-mail I received from a former student who recalled something I told her class in one of our last sessions: "Professor DeLong, do you remember when you told us that we are so competent interpersonally and socially that we can manipulate our environments to receive just the feedback, just the information, we want to receive just when we want to receive it from the person we want to receive it from? Well, it's true! I catch myself doing it all the time, particularly when I'm losing perspective."

We know the exact person to call when we want a particular response. We know that when we are discouraged a person's face comes to mind and we can predict what he or she will tell us. While it's a normal behavior, it will prevent you from moving from anxiety and fear to a more courageous and vulnerable place where change is possible.

The impulse to choose a "safe" confidant is powerful, and we may not even be conscious that this is what we're doing. Deep down inside, we worry that if someone tells us what he thinks of us and it's not flattering, it might shatter how we see ourselves. It may also call into question our significance, whether we make a difference to anyone—if they think we think too highly of ourselves or aren't strong managers, it's possible that we are contributing far less than we thought.

Yet these honest conversations have a huge upside. They push us to reflect on whether our lives have purpose and meaning. More to the point, they focus our attention on what is meaningful to us and how we contribute more than we know, in ways we might not have previously imagined. We never grasped that our ability to draw out the shyest members of our team is seen as a major contribution, that we're esteemed for our patience with and insight into employees who are reluctant to share their ideas. We would never have known this fact unless we had someone who was willing to tell us this. It's not just negatives that come out of these conversations but positives as well. When we have a network of straight talkers, we have a much better understanding of who we are within the organization.

Without these conversations, we simply create our own illusions (some of them accurate, but many not) that help us manage for that moment. They get us by. Over time this process of self-deception creates patterns. Others will come to the realization that we are not who we think we are. And if others know our true identities, we are in for a rude awakening. We may think of ourselves as kind dispensers of wisdom, but we'll be shocked to discover that our colleagues view us quite differently. Until that moment, we will believe the story that we have made up based on our history or old behaviors.

The SKS Form

When I was in graduate school, Phil Daniels, then a psychology professor at Brigham Young University, taught us about a feedback mechanism he called the SKS form. It was simply a process whereby we would ask others what we should *stop* (St), *keep* (K), and *start* (S) doing, given a particular role we might have as a teacher, friend, spouse, father, mother, etc. People are asked to fill in the blanks, limiting their entries to no more than three bullet points under each subheading.

Eventually I introduced the SKS process into faculty evaluations at universities, as well as performance appraisals on Wall Street. I've found it helps me as well as others avoid living in our fantasies of who we think we are. The specificity of knowing what we should quit, keep, and start doing anchors us in reality.

I would urge you to tell your support people about the SKS process and ask them to do a SKS for you regularly and hold you accountable for what they list. It's a simple tool, but a highly effective one. Too often, we may tell ourselves that we have to quit being such a micromanager (for instance), but our resolve to stop micromanaging gets lost in the activity of daily events. By having your support team respond to these three simple questions, invaluable feedback can be obtained. The questions are:

1. What should I stop doing?

2. What should I keep doing?

3. What should I start doing?

The SKS also counteracts our tendency to avoid seeking out other people's opinions of our attitudes and behaviors. When you are feeling the worst about yourself you don't ask for more feedback. You don't want to know. You use the excuse that you are already being tough on yourself so you don't need anyone else to be harsh. This rationale creates a vicious cycle where there is no need for you to learn of other views or ask for help. If you don't hear the hard truth from others, you don't have to acknowledge that it's real. The SKS process breaks the hold our illusions have on us. We probably intuitively know what we're doing wrong as well as right—there are few surprises in feedback— but the SKS approach brings things to the surface and forces us to confront them.

When you have your support team do an SKS, use the following questions to help you identify the behaviors that are keeping you stuck in the do-the-wrong-thing-well quadrant and the behaviors that will help you move to the do-the-right-thing-poorly quadrant:

Stop

- Are you hearing that you should quit doing something that you feel is a skill or strength?

- Is your first response that quitting this behavior will have catastrophic consequences?

- On reflection, is it possible that you've fallen into a behavioral rut? If you stop doing one thing, might you have an opportunity to try something new and different?

Keep

- Is there something you're doing right that people feel you should do more of?

- Have you been dismissive of this particular behavior or skill for some reason?

- What might happen if you used this "Keep" more? How might it impact your effectiveness and satisfaction with your job?

Start

- Are people recommending you do something that feels foreign or scary?

- What about it makes you anxious? Is it because you are afraid of looking like you don't know what you're doing?

- Why are people suggesting you start doing this new thing? What benefits do they feel will accrue to you, your group, or your organization?

Timing Is Everything

Driven professionals need support regularly and immediately. Unfortunately, many high-need-for-achievement people view support as something they should seek in a once-in-a-career emergency. While it certainly can be useful during crises, it is far more useful if it's received regularly in order to escape anxiety traps and gain the courage to be vulnerable and change. Similarly, seeking support days or weeks after a particular incident is fine, but obtaining it as close to a problematic event as possible increases the odds that this new information will result in a fresh perspective and new, more productive behaviors.

Let's look at both of these issues in a bit more depth, starting with the need to receive regular helpings of support.

Seek Support Frequently

In some companies, there are honest, no-holds-barred conversations between bosses and direct reports, but they only take place at year's end. Unlike frequent, more informal conversations, the year-end approach becomes an event that brings with it assumptions and expectations that can't be met. More important, it does little good to report on observations that took place nine months ago. If I tell a young faculty member in December that a number of students complained about an incident that took place in his classroom last May, he will probably respond with resentment and anger. The young academic thinks, "Why didn't you tell me what you observed last semester?" He begins to call into question the basic nature of the relationship; he wonders if there is other information or feedback that is not being shared. In the wake of this suspicion and fueled by his anger and resentment, he creates a story for himself that is probably not true. He'll tell himself that I have another agenda for sharing this information with him: that I'm jealous of the inroads he has made, or that I'm playing games with him because of my own insecurity. Thus, he doesn't have to deal with the reality.

Another problem is that year-end conversations are biased toward the previous two months. The majority of the year is not taken into consideration but, instead, recent incidents and performance issues receive priority.

A third downside is that little follow-up occurs after the yearly conversation has taken place. People are left to speculate about the outcome, how their career will be impacted by the feedback, whether there is a future for them at the company, and whether they have a mentor who takes them and their career seriously.

To avoid these problems, you should be proactive in seeking feedback regularly and routinely. Don't save up your questions and concerns for one marathon session at the end of the year. You'll find that taking advice and ideas in small increments is easier for you to digest. When people tell you that you should quit a certain behavior more than once and within different contexts, their point sinks in and you're more likely to take action on it.

Seek Support ASAP

You should also attempt to receive feedback within forty-eight hours of a spotlighted problem, issue, or concern. The forty-eight-hour rule means that when you do have a major conversation, whether at the end of the year or at another time, there are no surprises. Everything has been brought up and talked about shortly after it occurred. You should hold your boss, your mentor, your spouse, or anyone else in your support network accountable for "immediate transparency." The forty-eight-hour approach takes a lot of the sting out of negative feedback and gives you the emotional space necessary to learn from what you hear. Right after a challenging situation or traumatic incident, you want to talk about it; it's on your mind, you have a ton of questions, and the event is fresh enough in your mind that you're clear on what took place. You're willing to tolerate constructive criticism because you're eager to know what you might do differently and better. If you have this same conversation with your support team a few weeks or months later, you'll be far less interested in hearing anything negative, since the incident no longer is of great concern to you. You've moved on to other things, so you're less open to what you hear.

Ask for Feedback Before It's Given

If you have built up a network of trusted colleagues and "outsiders," you are much more likely to make yourself vulnerable and use what you learn to change behavioral patterns. One day, as we were thinking through a curriculum design for a potential course, executive coach Jeffrey Kerr asked me, "When was the last time you invited someone to question your assumptions?" I'd also like to think that I create a climate in which those with whom I interact feel comfortable enough to question me and my assumptions. Perhaps I talk a good game. Maybe those around me don't feel like they can disagree with me. Maybe it's time for me to do a better job of creating my network of trusted advisers and raising this issue for discussion.

The question Kerr posed to me brought back memories of a conversation I had many years ago at the Sloan School of Management at MIT with one my mentors, Edgar Schein. Schein told me that he had learned over the years that it was fruitless to give anyone advice or feedback unless they asked for it. Giving advice did no good. If anything, he maintained, it hurt the situation. The other person simply would become more defensive. He admonished me to create the kind of climate where individuals felt safe enough to ask for feedback.

A team of trusted advisers keeps us from closing ourselves off to our self-perceived reality. They provide us with a resource that we're not afraid to access; we feel sufficiently comfortable with them to ask for help. This is especially true when we're under stress or struggling with something. That's when we're most likely to retreat to our "realities" of who we are as professionals or managers; that's when we're most likely to cling to unproductive or dysfunctional behaviors. If we have a team of advisers, we can discuss the situation with them and they can jolt us back to reality and help us see what we're doing or likely to do. That's the way we can overcome our fears and gain the courage to be vulnerable, learn, and change.

Once you have a purpose and a team in place, you're on the path to change. In the next chapter, I'll discuss what steps you need to take on this path and why they seem frightening but are actually easier to embrace than you think.

CHAPTER TWELVE

Don't Blink

IF YOU BLINK, YOU BECOME INDECISIVE, uncertain, and passive. When high-need-for-achievement professionals become mired in anxiety-producing traps, they tend to think too much and act too little. In other words, individuals won't try something new, will shy away from an innovative approach, or will decide not to make the commitment they promised themselves they'd make. Blinking means hesitating and falling back on old behaviors because of fear of the unknown. Blinking means holding on to the past, to the stories you've told yourself that keep you imprisoned in old behaviors and ways of thinking and of seeing yourself. Blinking, essentially, is refusing to pull the trigger when deep inside you know it needs to be pulled.

Blinking takes no time at all. And that is how long it takes for many individuals to sabotage their own efforts. All sorts of professionals become caught by that split-second of doubt and uncertainty, and they don't act. They hear the clarion call of resistance. They hold fast to those beliefs that keep them stuck. I'm not suggesting that everyone should plunge into every opportunity without assessing the risks; fly-ing without a net is different than flying blind. Flying without a net works only when you have prepared, taken time to reflect, and decided that vulnerability and courage are better alternatives.

The advice proffered here, though, is that there are times in every driven professional's life when it is necessary to act decisively. You need to be prepared to face into a situation that makes you anxious and that may entail some risks, and yet move forward with the cer-tainty that it's the right thing to do. The courage not to blink wells inside based on the innate faith that you will get through it.

How can you possess this don't-blink attitude? Let's look at some examples of high achievers who have mastered and used it to their advantage.

Rick Cohen Didn't Blink Twice

As a twenty-eight-year-old college graduate, Rick Cohen, now chair-man of C&S Wholesale Grocers—the seventh-largest privately held company in the United States—found himself working as a supervisor at the family wholesale grocery business in Worcester, Massachusetts. The company had big problems: it had previously dealt with a flood that had ruined most of their products, and had been confronted by unions time and time again.

Cohen's father Lester met him one day on the loading docks and asked him to take over the business and run the company. What do you do at age twenty-eight when you see your family business hang-ing by a thread—sixty-five years of family history in the balance? You think about your grandfather, Israel, and know that he started this enterprise in 1912—and know that despite your fears and uncertain-ties, this is the right thing for you to do. Cohen said yes. And then he decided to move the company to Vermont, an even bolder move that entailed both risk and potential reward. He would bet the business on moving to a free state where unions didn't have such a strong hold. He would move to a state where taxes and state governance weren't as suffocating. And he would build a large distribution center that initially wasn't even near capacity, knowing that if he didn't fill the center and get more customers the company would go under. And he would have family members watching every step.

Cohen pulled it off. Twenty years later, looking back on how he did it, he said, "If I showed doubts myself then we would have failed. If I had shown doubt in any way, what do you think the employees would have thought? If I had waffled in any way, what would they think about their leader? There are certain times that you simply have to have faith in yourself and in others. Shortly after we moved we received a call from A&P that would change us forever. They said that they wanted us to handle the majority of their business. They wanted us to take over their wholesale distribution. It would move our business from being a $250 million business to a $450 million business. We said yes. We said that we could do their business at the highest-quality levels. I wasn't sure at all if we could do it. But I knew that we always underestimate what we can accomplish. And we did it."

Cohen made another key bet in the late '80s, when the company was struggling with quality issues, high turnover, high accident rates, and growing competition. All its metrics focused on individual performance. Whoever loaded the most cases made the most money. If a case was missing from where it belonged on the racks, the selector would pick up a case of whatever was closest and throw it on his pallet. By the time the mistake was uncovered at a given store, it was impossible to track the error. Needless to say, customers suffered because the metrics were not aligned with the customer proposition. And customers were furious.

C&S had just won the A&P work, which made a bad situation potentially catastrophic. A&P was the biggest customer by far that C&S had taken on. Up to this point, all its customers had been independent operators; C&S had intentionally stayed away from larger customers. And the timing couldn't have been worse. It was late October, and the holiday season faced Cohen and his workers. Cohen had been contemplating whether or not team-based work groups would be more effective. No one in the industry had ever tried such a thing at that time, although research was emerging that teams could produce more in less time given the right rewards and metrics. After meeting with some senior producers, Cohen decided to move toward a team-based system, one that would either transform or bring down the business. Five hundred workers devised a system to divide everyone into teams. Within two weeks the company was moving from an individual to a teamwork philosophy. Productivity began to skyrocket. Accidents plummeted. Selectors were making more money than ever. C&S was able to cost-effectively reduce the number of teams because they were becoming more productive and effective.

This one bet by Cohen to move from individual to team performance changed the nature of the wholesale game in the United States. Competitors wanted to know how Cohen was able to convince his workers to make the change. He commented, "It's funny what can happen when you include and involve and give workers more responsibility." Nearly twenty years later, C&S is one of the last great wholesale companies standing, with revenues of over $20 billion. Cohen continues to take informed and prudent risks that have transformed the wholesale business. When competitors visit one of C&S's myriad distribution centers around the country, they make the same remark during each visit: "I could never get my workers to work like this. These workers are athletes. It's an inspiration to see their commitment to their work, each other, and the company."

What lessons can high-need-for-achievement professionals draw from Cohen's experiences? I realize that many of you aren't in Rick Cohen's position and faced with the prospect of saving the family business or transforming the entire structure of your organizations. But if you're a driven professional, you're faced with situations where you can either blink or not blink. You find that you've been doing things one way for a long time, and that to move away from your traditional behaviors or approach is challenging. Then, you're presented with an opportunity to do something differently. How do you overcome your fears and seize the opportunity? Do what Cohen did and try the following:

- Combine logic with instinct to do what is right. Cohen wasn't sure that the move to Vermont would pay off, but despite the radical nature of the strategy, it made sense in terms of lower costs. And his gut told him to do it.

- Be willing to bet the farm if you truly believe in a given action or change. Cohen bet the family business knowing that a team structure would make it or break it. His strong belief in this move provided the energy and commitment to make it happen. Belief is a powerful tool, and driven professionals who act on it find it easier not to blink.

How To Go Forward When Your Fear Says Stop

In her first year of medical school our daughter Sara was diagnosed with lymphoma. Ironically, it was diagnosed during her oncology course, and she found out her test results on her birthday. Over the ensuing year she went through the normal regimen of chemotherapy. It was a miserable experience. Of course, she lost her hair. I remember going with her to pick up the wig she had ordered. One look in the mirror was enough for her to decide that a scarf or bandana would be a better alternative. Throughout this whole ordeal, Sara would decide to keep going through medical school, only to lose the courage that it would take to make it through. At one point she turned to me and stated, "I'm going to quit deciding whether or not to delay school. I'm just going to get over myself, my self-consciousness, and get back in school."

People who refuse to blink draw on some inner resource that provides them with the courage and motivation to take a chance. Certainly this ability comes naturally to a lucky few, but the rest of us have to develop this resource. Some people can do it on their own. Earl, for instance, worked in his family's business for years, and he was expected to take over when his father retired. Though he had four other siblings, they were all women and had no interest in the business. A patriarchal company, the family business had been started by Earl's great-grandfather and handed down to his grandfather. Earl felt a lot of pressure to follow in their footsteps—more internal pressure than from his father.

Yet after Earl graduated with an MBA, he became interested in medicine, in part because of the illness of one of his sisters. Over the years, he talked with his wife and others about going back to medical school, but there was always some reason not to. In his spare time, Earl studied biology and chemistry textbooks, telling himself it was just for his own amusement. He decided to take the MCATs, and did very well. Then, more out of curiosity than anything else (or so he told himself), he applied to medical schools. One of them accepted him, and Earl was faced with a tough decision.

It would be so easy to continue his current work. Though he didn't love his job, he liked it and was good at it. He also was very well compensated and had time to take great vacations with his wife and kids. Earl knew that going back to medical school at age thirty-six would be difficult in many ways—not the least of which was the conversation he would have to have with his father. But there were also his wife and kids to consider; he would have to explain to them how the drop in income would affect their lifestyle—it might even mean selling their large house and moving into a smaller one. And it also meant admitting to himself that he had made a mistake all these years, that he should have gone to medical school ten years earlier. As a proud man with a healthy ego, it was difficult for Earl to admit that he had made this earlier decision. It was much easier rationalizing the decision as he had done, telling himself all the reasons why medical school was a pipe dream.

Earl deferred admission for one year, and then took a weekend by himself at the family cabin in the woods. He walked a lot, thought a lot, and by the end of the weekend, he hadn't blinked. At one point, he admitted to himself that he was afraid; that he was scared not only of going to medical school but of discovering that he didn't like it after all or that he wasn't good at medicine. For some reason, that realization muted his fear. It helped him think more clearly about his decision. And in that moment, he resolved to go to med school. When he returned, he sat down with his father and informed him of his choice. Though his father was disappointed, he was not as angry as Earl had anticipated. When he told his wife, she asked him a lot of difficult questions related to money, but after putting everything down on paper and talking with a financial consultant, they figured out a strategy that made sense.

Once Earl committed to the school, he felt relieved. Though he knew it would be difficult transitioning from a business executive to a neophyte medical student, he couldn't wait to make that transition. He was a high-need-for-achievement professional, but he needed to achieve in a different field—a field that would provide him with the meaning and fulfillment he craved.

As Earl's and Rick Cohen's stories illustrate, not blinking is often a matter of having the courage to face a difficult decision, admit your fear, but move forward anyway. While Earl faced into a major career decision and Cohen confronted a major choice for the future of his company, many other types of decisions exist where a clear, steady gaze is required. If you work for a major corporation, for instance, you may need to turn down a promotion that you know will confine you to the do-the-wrong-thing-well quadrant; or you may need to volunteer for a team or assignment where you have a good chance of failing but an even better chance of learning a new skill or gaining valuable knowledge.

When you read about it here, not blinking seems like a relatively simple action to execute. In the real world, however, it can be tremendously challenging. Like most high-need-for-achievement professionals, you yearn for that promotion and you can't stand the thought of making a mistake. Not blinking often means ignoring your short-term need for obvious symbols of success as well as your fear of looking bad in front of others.

To help you execute a no-blink approach to crucial decisions, here are some steps that might help:

1. Face into your fear: Be up-front with yourself about what is keeping you stuck in quadrant 1 and what is so scary about quadrant 3; acknowledge how you feel safe and comfortable practicing a skill that you know you're good at and how you will feel vulnerable and uncomfortable doing something you're not yet good at.

2. Use your achievement goal to overcome your fear: What do you yearn to accomplish, and what sacrifices are worth making to accomplish it? When you focus on the future objective rather than the difficult present action or decision, you give yourself a powerful incentive not to blink.

3. Consider weakness and uncertainty as the price you must pay for learning and growth: See these feelings as a necessary cost rather than as avoidable at all costs. It provides a useful shift of frame; it offers a clear benefit for enduring your discomfort and not blinking.

4. Use a negative sanction: Picture yourself blinking and therefore doing what you're currently doing five years from now, ten

years from now. As a driven professional, the last thing you want is to remain stuck in your career. If you blink and refuse to take a chance on new learning and growth, you're likely to remain stuck. Use this image as another source of motivation when you're facing a tough choice.

Now let's look at another tactic that you can use when that inner voice of conservatism in your head tells you to blink and you require another voice to tell you not to.

Use Your Inner Circle

In chapter 11, I discussed the importance of forming a small network of individuals on whom you can rely. Sometimes professionals establish these relationships but then don't take full advantage of them. Too often, they rely on these relationships only for social reasons—people to go to lunch with, for instance—or for relatively minor career and business advice. If, however, you've built a network of people who are insightful, empathetic, and absolutely honest in their feedback, then you need to trust them during turning points. These are the situations in which you need support in order not to blink.

Research demonstrates that change doesn't happen alone. Even though we are ultimately responsible for the change within, we need a helping hand to grab us when we hit a rough patch. When we can confide in someone about our anxieties and hear a voice of reason and truth in response, we gain confidence in our decision and stop asking ourselves scores of paralyzing "what-if" questions.

Rick Cohen at C&S, for instance, relied on Reuben Harris, a consultant and friend. Harris asked early and often whether Cohen was moving in the right direction. That doesn't mean that Harris told Cohen not to blink. But he did tell him that there was no way to succeed if he second-guessed himself each time he tried something new.

A network of friends and internal consultants keep you grounded and aware of where you are going or when you are off track. And you know that they will be there for you. They are not like business partners who are interested in you being successful every time out. Instead, they are there to challenge and support you. When they see you manipulating your environment to hear and see only what you want to hear and see, they call you on it.

In chapter 11, I noted how we often rely on those individuals for feedback who will provide us with what we want to hear. If we do that in situations in which we absolutely cannot blink, they probably won't be able to keep us from doing it. The whole point is knowing that you have people who will tell the honest truth about anything significant you plan to do, and that they'll tell it to you even if they know you would prefer to hear something different.

I mentioned earlier in the book that I emphasize to students that they could manipulate their environment to receive the feedback they wanted whenever they wanted to feel a certain way. If they were discouraged, they knew the individual to call who would lift their spirits. If they wanted other types of feedback that supported the way they saw themselves, they could call a particular sibling or parent. But this wouldn't be the feedback that would help them change and grow or make the tough decisions that needed to be made. If they chose to manipulate their environment, they only supported their preconceived notions about what they wanted to do. And many times, these notions were about not changing, about not tackling new challenges, about maintaining the status quo, and finding a psychologically safe rut and staying there. In other words, their accommodating friends would allow them to blink. They would enable them to continue to remain passive when they should take action.

I've remonstrated with myself in these pages about why I waited so long before asking my children how I could have been a better parent and my fear that they would respond by painting an unflattering picture of me as a parent. Finally, when I mustered the courage to ask them what I was doing well or poorly, I was surprised by their responses. Joanna told me she wanted me to read her more books when I came home. She liked the fact that I wrestled with her and took her friends to the ice cream store. Catharine wanted me to go more often with her to riding practice. And Sara wanted to go on a trip on my Harley-Davidson. These were not huge demands. They did not deliver the news in a hostile manner. They didn't take much time in delivering the news—they just said it almost in passing and then moved on to some other activity or project. It wasn't a big deal. Yet, I had feared having the conversation. I was disappointed that I waited so long because of the story I had created in my head about what I would hear. More important, I had been afraid that I would have to make some radical transformation in who I was. The fears and apprehensions within controlled my behavior in ways that reduced my learning and growth.

If I would have asked them this question earlier, I would have been able to make the changes they requested without blinking. Essentially, I would have resolved to spend more time with them to do the things they wanted to do. My daughters formed a terrific network, but I didn't access it as soon as I might have. It's no good having a great network of people unless you use it.

When I joined Morgan Stanley years ago, John Mack hired me based mainly on intuition. He didn't want a typical human resources viewpoint; he wanted someone who saw organizations from a different perspective than typical bankers. He wanted someone who could give him insights that might mitigate his blind spots as president of Morgan Stanley. So he hired this professor to focus on human capital and the development of the organization and individuals within it. Most important, he wanted a truth speaker. That would prove to be the most valuable role I played while working there.

The trouble is that most of us say we want to know the ways of change, we want to know our blind spots, we want to be able to stare unblinking at a challenge and embrace it. Yet we go back to old ways that lock us into familiar, dysfunctional patterns. We blink and return to the way we've always done things rather test a new behavior or develop a new understanding. Mentors, friends, partners, significant others, therapists, and colleagues all can provide the support we require so that we move forward through our fear.

So when you're facing a challenge or decision that requires you not to blink, you need to talk to your key advisers in a very specific way. Do not describe the situation you've encountered in a way that encourages them to encourage you to play it safe. Even straight-talking colleagues and friends may be swayed by your fear and suggest you avoid making yourself vulnerable. Instead, describe the blinking situation this way:

- Explain what you're fearful about, but also describe how a given decision might help you learn, grow, and change in positive ways.

- Frame the situation in terms of the quadrants introduced in figure 2-2—say that you want to move from the do-the-wrong-thing-well quadrant to the do-the-right-thing-poorly quadrant.

- Ask them point blank if they think that this is a situation where it's worthwhile to be courageously vulnerable, to take the risk of looking uncertain or wrong in order to change in a positive way.

Know When to Say Yes and When to Say No

The ongoing process of moving through our uncertainties was captured brilliantly by Freeman Dyson, a theoretical physicist and mathematician and a former professor at Princeton. Dyson was asked to speak at

Brigham Young University in the early '90s. I remember him as small in stature but bold and thoughtful. As he closed his speech to the student body he reflected, "What I'm really saying is that the essence of life is when to say yes and when to say no." He further explained, "Say yes to adventure and no to folly. And only you can know the difference."

Not blinking does not mean that you have license to be reckless or insensitive or hurtful to others. Not blinking gives you the right to seek self-awareness, learn how to regulate your behavior, and understand situations that confront you. As you develop a sense of who you are as a person and a professional, you become more and more aware of the difference between adventure and folly. Not blinking is something that takes practice to be good at. It's not just a one-time experience, but something that is continuous. Over time, you'll find that you'll become much better at both knowing the situations when you shouldn't blink and having the courage to stare wide-eyed into challenges that used to make you blink or even turn away in fear. Through this process of taking on challenging tasks and overcoming your anxieties, you will gain further assurance of when to blink and when not to.

CHAPTER THIRTEEN

Ask Someone to Dance

A FEW YEARS AGO, a friend recounted a story told by Alec Horni-man at the University of Virginia. Horniman drew a picture of a basketball court on the blackboard. After drawing the rectangular diagram, though, Horniman began talking about attending a high school dance after a Friday night basketball game in the middle of winter. He described the dances he attended while growing up.

The students head to the gymnasium lobby as the custodians sweep the floor after the game and set up for the dance. The setup is the same wherever you attend one of these high school dances. There is someone managing the music. Parents or teachers are managing the refreshments. The lights are dimmed before the students reenter the gym. The younger high school girls enter the gym as a pack, as do the younger boys. The upper-grade boys and girls may have paired off and attend as couples. But the vast majority of students attend with same-gender groups. The girls enter and begin to hug one wall or they go the restroom. The boys head for the food. Some boys never end up dancing because they are too shy and self-conscious or they are too cool or already stoned.

The challenge is how to begin to get these reluctant students to dance. Who goes first? Who will lead and be the first ones on the floor? Parents or teachers can try and start the ball rolling, but it generally doesn't work—no teenager wants to join adults in a dance. What about the most popular kids? They are too invested in image to be the first ones to take the risk of doing anything first.

Horniman said that the role of the leader in an organization is to create a climate where employees at every level possess the courage and the motivation to be the first one on the proverbial dance floor. Each person needs to process the experience in real time. Each individual has to decide if it is worth it to move past the butterflies, the self-consciousness, and the internal tug of war and be the first one to walk to the center of the dance floor.

This isn't about mustering the internal fortitude to take a bold action once a year. It's about developing everyday courage. It's about developing an attitude that says that life is worth taking the risk.

At this point, you may be saying to yourself, "But what if my colleagues will criticize my efforts? What if my organizational culture is such that it frowns upon taking risks?" My first response is that in some instances, ambitious, driven professionals project their own fears onto their bosses and organizations; they assume that because they're anxious about heading to the center of the court, so too are their colleagues and managers. In other instances, bosses and cultures may very well frown on people who make dumb decisions and who act in ways that are ill conceived and ill considered, but they very much want their people to learn, change, and grow. Sometimes, of course, they're right—they work for status quo–maintaining. Some risk-averse companies want to keep their people confined to the do-the-wrong-thing-well quadrant in figure 2-2. In these situations, you may want to consider other work alternatives if remaining in place means remaining stuck where you are in perpetuity.

Whatever the reason that driven professionals decide to sit out the dance, being an observer rather than a participant has further consequences. When we stand on the sidelines, we become passive onlookers as others dance. We learn only to focus on how others are living life. Even worse, this observation commits us to passivity. When we leave the dance at the end of the evening we feel a little less satisfied, a little less soothed, even a little sad and wanting something more. We leave with some "I wish I would have's." We also reinforce our belief that others experience life in a more dynamic way and that something prevents us from doing the same. We may also find ourselves gradually being more critical of others even though we in reality are envious of their courage.

While we watch others dance we find ourselves having conversations with ourselves that are not positively reinforcing. They are just the opposite. They are more about inadequacies, about weaknesses, about how we don't measure up. We don't realize when we're at the dance that we're doing something negative, that our problems are self-created. We don't like owning up to the fact that we had one more chance to jump in and we decided to watch others make the leap. And we are one more evening away from learning how to dance, instead chalking up one more evening and experience that makes us feel like we are less than whole. And each time we watch the others, the more difficult it becomes to step out onto the dance floor the next time.

Whether we're adolescents trying to gather the courage to ask a girl to dance or driven professionals trying to take on a fresh challenge, we need to overcome our anxiety, gather our courage, and allow ourselves to be vulnerable. It's the only way we're going to move from one quadrant to the next; it's the only way we're going to grow. This is true whether we're just starting out in our careers or have been working for a considerable period of time. In fact, the older we become, the more difficult it is to try something new; we settle for our comfortable routines. We may have started our careers dynamic and full of interest in learning and developing, but the older we became, the more self-conscious we are about admitting we don't know something or about trying and not looking good in the process. We cling to structure and routine, and we become defensive when others recommend change.

Be aware, then, that this unwillingness to dance can happen to you. When you're starting out in your career, you're more like the teenager at the dance, terrified of doing something you've never done before or looking foolish. If you're older and more experienced, you're scared of showing weakness or making a mistake. You believe someone in a managerial or leadership position must present a strong, even invulnerable, front to the outside world. In essence, you revert to your adolescent mind-set despite your accomplishments.

The first step toward the dance floor, then, involves making yourself aware of the situations in the past where you refused to dance and the price you paid for this inaction. To that end, try the following exercise:

1. Recall an instance when you had the opportunity to make a difference at work: an opportunity to be part of a cutting-edge team, the chance to take on a stretch assignment, a situation in which your decision could have changed the work dynamic in your group for the better. But in this instance, you didn't capitalize on the opportunity or decision in front of you. With hindsight, you know what you should have done, but you didn't do it.

2. On a sheet of paper, list all the thoughts and feelings that prevented you from taking the right action. For instance, one thought might be: "My analysis told me that it was smarter to do nothing rather than expose myself to criticism." Or: "I was afraid of looking bad in front of my boss."

3. On that same piece of paper, list all the potential positive outcomes that might have been produced by taking the action you refused to take. What learning might you have gained? What skills might you have acquired? How might it have made you a better manager and leader?

This exercise isn't for the faint of heart. Just as many of us still regret not asking that one girl to dance, many of us are sorry that we didn't ask for the transfer or take on the tough assignment. But recognizing this regret is crucial. Once you're aware of it and reflect on it, you're less likely to make the same mistake again.

Spit

A good friend served on the National Ski Patrol for the State of Oregon for many years. Bill spent most of his time on Mt. Hood helping those in need on the ski slopes. In 1986 there was a tragic accident on Mt. Hood. On June 26, fifteen teenagers from a private school in Portland, Oregon, were hiking on Mt. Hood and were caught in a storm above the timberline. These young hikers were not prepared for such an event. They didn't know that expert mountain climbers preparing to climb in the Himalayas practiced on Mt. Hood because the mountain was known for its unpredictable weather. This storm struck just five days after the summer solstice. The students were wearing shorts and short-sleeve shirts with very little protection for inclement weather. They carried little water or extra food. They had no clue how to find direction in freezing rain and snow with wind blowing the snow horizontally. They were lost for three days. Only a few survived.

On many occasions I've queried Bill about bad-weather survival skills, and I was especially interested in his advice about how to survive an avalanche. Bill taught me that the reality is that virtually no one out-skis an avalanche.

If you are skiing and caught in an avalanche, the first step is to release your bindings and knock off your skis; if they're on when you're buried under the snow, they may anchor you in place and prevent your escape. Once your skis are off, the snow will carry you down the mountain and you will be freer to deal with your situation. Once you quit moving, create an air space around your mouth by clearing away some of the snow and make a space to breathe by cupping your hands. Once you cup your hands, you spit. Why? The key to survival is to find out which way is up and which way is down. You have to rely on the law of gravity. If you've slid with the snow and been buried in it, you don't know which way is up or down—and that means you won't know what direction you need to dig. When you spit the saliva will travel. Gravity pulls the spit down, and then you know to dig up.

Bill said he had seen over four people who were less than a foot from the surface of the snow who began digging in the wrong direction. They could have survived. They could have lived another day had they known about this simple survival rule.

It's the small, commonsense things that make all the difference. Many times, high-need-for-achievers become so wrapped up in the big picture that they fail to take the small, practical steps that lead to big achievements. Return to the dance metaphor for a moment. You're going to have trouble getting up the nerve to ask someone to dance if you focus on approaching the most popular girl in school and imagining all the reasons she might turn you down. You can increase the odds of asking her, though, if you do a number of small things first: talk to her in school; determine how the conversation went; sit at the same lunch table as her and strike up another conversation; visualize what you're going to say to her when you approach her at the dance.

These small, commonsense tactics are like spitting when you're buried by an avalanche: they increase the odds of your taking the right action and achieving your objective.

How does the "spit" tactic translate into career and work situations?

Here are just a handful of commonsense actions that ambitious professionals can take to help get themselves out of paralysis and onto new paths of learning and growth:

- Invite the boss for lunch, drinks, golf, or other casual get-together: In other words, get the boss in a casual setting where it's not so difficult to express how you really feel about your current assignments or the type of tasks you'd really like to do.

- Ask a what-if question: Talk to your mentor, boss, coach, or any other influential person in your life and pose a hypothetical situation that involves yourself and a significant change in how, where, or why you work. For instance: "What if I worked in India for a year?" or "What if I took a sabbatical?" These what-ifs catalyze discussions that may lead to major changes in your professional life.

- Decide to learn something new: Sign up for a training session, attend a workshop, or apprentice yourself informally to someone in your organization who can teach you something you don't know. Learning is a catalyst for growth and change, and though it may not be apparent how a given learning experience will facilitate growth and change, take it on faith that acquiring knowledge and skills opens up doors that now are closed.

Like spitting when you're buried in snow, none of these common-sense acts are profound. But they are just the sort of small steps that high-need-for-achievement professionals ignore, and thus they fail to get up the nerve to do something different.

Changing the Medium Reduces the Tedium

After completing his doctorate in organizational behavior, Steve accepted an offer to join the faculty of a prestigious university. While driving cross country in a U-Haul truck, he began to remind himself of all the challenges that lay before him. And it seemed as though the list got longer with each passing mile. By the time he arrived in the university town he felt as though he was walking in quicksand.

Before deciding where to live, Steve moved into university housing. When he woke up early the next morning Steve felt as if the weight of the world rested on his shoulders. He began to wonder whether he had made the right career decision. He wondered how he would be received by his colleagues at the university. He wondered whether or not he would be able to teach effectively and gain the students' respect. He wondered how his wife would adjust to the new surroundings away from her family and support system. He wondered whether she would be able to find a job in her field. He wondered how he would adjust to the realities of the life of a professor.

He wondered how he would take care of his aging parents who lived across the country from him. He wondered whether he would be able to publish his doctoral work and gain credibility in the academic world. He wondered whether he and his wife would be able to find an affordable house that wouldn't need too much repair and renovation. He wondered how he would be able to help his brother, who needed financial help, when his starting salary wasn't that high. He wondered whether he and his wife would be able to find a good doctor to assist them as they planned for their second child. He wondered whether he would have the time to exercise with all the other demands that rested on his shoulders.

When Steve woke up on that first morning he rolled into a tight ball and wouldn't get out of bed. He called to his wife and asked if he could have just a few more minutes to lie there. The few minutes turned into a few hours and then a few days. Steve was literally paralyzed by his anxieties. There was no way that he could face the challenges of the days ahead, let alone the next few hours, without being overwhelmed.

Steve's wife called his best friend and a doctor. His best friend drove six hours and showed up in Steve's room. He took him by the hand and slowly helped him out of bed. He opened up the front door of the rented house and encouraged him to take small steps down the street. His friend continued to walk and talk with him for two hours. When they returned he drove Steve to the doctor.

The doctor listened. He offered Steve some advice, the main element being that he needed to depend on his family, friends, and colleagues for support to get him over this rough patch. He also assured him that he would succeed. And in fact, Steve did succeed, albeit in increments. He made it through that first day, and then the next, and went back to teaching and made it through the first week and the first month. Finally, he finished the first semester successfully.

Steve's case may be extreme, but it illustrates the challenge of doing something new and the obstacles that get in our way. We may not lie in bed for days because of our anxieties, but we may suffer from the same sort of inability to take action when action is necessary. How do we find the courage to change? How do we rise from our metaphorical beds and do something that is unfamiliar and challenging? Here's how: when you see yourself in danger of falling into comfortable patterns, make the effort to do the behavioral opposite of what you've been doing.

Over the years I have looked for highly technical interventions when trying to figure out how to get individuals over stasis and into the process of change, and consultant Ann Harriet Buck's concepts strike me as a good starting point. She suggests that when individuals feel stuck and experience psychological paralysis, they need to think about contrasts. She recommends beginning the process by doing the opposite of whatever you are doing. For Steve it meant moving—he had to get off the bed and get his feet in motion to combat his paralysis. For another person, it might mean slowing down and being more self-reflective if she has been trapped in a hyperactive mode. Buck simplifies it by pushing individuals to focus on contrasts:

- If you have been sitting, stand.

- If you have been standing, sit.

- If you are been traveling, stay home.

- If you have been home, travel.

- If you have been teaching, learn.

- If you have been learning, teach.

- If you have been talking, listen.

- If you have been listening, talk.[1]

If we translate this advice to high-need-for-achievement professionals, some common advice might be:

- If you have been playing it safe, take a risk.

- If you have been only working on tasks with which you're comfortable, take on a discomforting assignment.

- If you have been only listening to a small circle of advisers, bring in outsiders.

- If you have been focusing on short-term goals, think long term.

- If you have been a command-and-control leader, invite others into the decision-making process and listen more than you have ever listened.

You get the idea. Be aware that we all are being called upon to change in ways that are foreign to us. We can no longer maintain the status quo and expect to prosper in our organizations. To avoid being like Steve, we must be courageous enough to do something different than what we are doing.

Create Sacred Time

A few years ago a well-recognized CEO visited Harvard Business School. He advised the students to take time for family and friends as they made their way into the corporate world and started to advance their careers. One story he told generated a strong reaction. The executive mentioned that despite his busy work schedule over the years, he had a successful marriage and a good family life because he had committed an hour and a half each Sunday afternoon to be with his family.

When the guest left, I asked the students for their reactions. They couldn't believe that this leader actually thought that personal happiness was attained by sharing so little time with family. I followed up their criticism by asking them to write down the time in the last week where they had spent an hour and a half with those individuals closest to them. Students began to get defensive, protesting that it wasn't a fair request because they were in a tough graduate program and they had to commit everything to school. Some students actually believed that they would have much more time once they left school and entered the world of work.

Few driven professionals block out time to focus on the most important people in their lives. And often unintentional neglect withers those relationships on the vine. When no time is held sacred for these critical relationships, the consequences can be subtle but long-lasting. In very small, unambiguous ways, these relationships begin to erode without our even recognizing the process that is taking place. Block out time. Make the sacred time part of your agenda. Commit to turning off your PDAs. Commit to unplugging the phone and focusing just on the relationship at hand.

Do it not just for the sake of people you care most about but for your professional growth. The loner who has few friends or meaningful relationships will find it especially difficult to get up the nerve to ask someone to dance. When we're secure in the relationships that matter most, it's far easier to take chances at work, to embrace new experiences, to tackle challenging assignments, to adjust our management and leadership styles. Knowing that you can count on the people you care about the most provides a foundation for taking chances and not agonizing about the risks. When we're at loose ends personally—when we're having trouble with our children, or we're separating or divorcing, or we're feuding with other family members—we tend to want to keep things simple and easy at work. So we stick to the tried and true and limit the "noise" in our professional lives. When things are good personally, on the other hand, we're feeling good about ourselves and have more energy and confidence to take on new challenges.

Take a moment and think about whether you're making time for the people you care most about. I know all the excuses that high achievers give: *I'm always on the road; I work seven days a week; I don't have time for a family vacation this summer; I'm working on the biggest project in the organization; my boss is counting on me to come through.*

While all these excuses may be valid in one sense, they're not valid in another. If you can't carve out a reasonable time to be with the people you most care about, what's the point? Perhaps more to the point, how do you expect to muster the confidence to take the risk that will catapult you to a higher level of achievement? Without the support of friends and family, you probably won't pull the trigger when that big opportunity comes. You'll want to play it safe since, consciously or not, you're thinking, "If I fail at this task at which I don't have all the knowledge and skill I need, what do I have left?"

I understand how much work and success means to you, and how hard you work. I'm not suggesting that you should never work late or always attend every family function. You have to strike a balance. Consider, too, that this balance varies from individual to individual. We are all made differently, so I'm not trying to dictate how many hours we should all spend with our significant others, our children, and our friends.

Each of us gets to choose the method for growth. Each of us gets the chance to define the scope and scale of the adventure. We get to figure out the pacing and sequencing of our adventure. Most important, we get to experience what it feels like to come alive again after we have had our first dance after sitting out so many.

CHAPTER FOURTEEN

Returning to Rushmore

IT'S BEEN NEARLY TWENTY YEARS SINCE I first set my eyes on Mt. Rushmore. In Daisy Wademan's book *Remember Who You Are*, I tell the story of the memorable trip I took when my daughter Catharine so convincingly asked me to visit the monument in South Dakota. We lived nine hundred miles from the monument. Most important, Catharine wanted to take the Harley-Davidson—she would think up any excuse to get on the back of the bike. Even when I told her how long the trip would take, it didn't register to an eleven-year-old. We decided to go and left early on an August morning.

The story unfolded in a surprising way. Once we arrived, after two days on the road, we looked up at the four men in stone—George Washington, Thomas Jefferson, Abraham Lincoln, and Theodore Roosevelt—leaders who had made a significant impact in the history of the United States. Catharine asked me why these four men had been chosen. I responded by explaining some of the attributes shared by the four great presidents. And I also tried to supply my own theories to compensate for my lack of historical knowledge and also putting it in language I thought my daughter would appreciate. I told her that when they were frightened they did their work anyway. I told her that when some people didn't believe in them or said bad things about them they went ahead and were courageous. I described how they had all tried to make the country better through their efforts, and that they had all wanted to make the lives of the citizens of the country better. I pointed out that each had fears whether they could accomplish their tasks, but they all pushed through fears to accomplish their goals. I highlighted that at the end of the day they all wanted to make a difference in the lives of others through courageous acts over a long period of time. That's when the conversation took an unexpected twist.

Catharine looked up at me and asked in the most sincere and straightforward way, "Dad, do you make a difference?" I met the question with silence. I'd never had anyone ask me that question. I had asked myself, but only superficially and only momentarily. Now, someone who I valued and was so impressionable had called my bluff. She wanted to know what my assessment was of me. After only a few moments that felt like days, I responded, "Catharine, I hope I do, but I need to think more about the answer to the question. But I really hope I make a difference."

All the way home from South Dakota to Utah, over each of those nine hundred miles, I pondered her question. I wondered if I was really making a difference in life or whether I was just touching the surface, skimming along the top in a way that only looked as if I was doing real work. Through Cody, Wyoming, and Yellowstone Park, through the Grand Tetons, and through Star Valley, Wyoming, I kept asking myself whether or not I was really making a difference or just going through the motions. Did I matter? And did my work matter, or was I just trying to keep myself looking important and industrious? Catharine asked me that question in 1991. And the answer to the question helped precipitate a journey that I continue to be on. This query helped me stop and really think about significance. I wondered if I had created stories to justify what I did or did not do in my life. I wondered whether or not my efforts were really having any impact at all on others other than in a superficial manner.

That is one of the first times that I really began to understand what it might take to move from the left side of the 2 × 2 matrix shown in figure 2-2, and the importance of doing the right thing poorly before we can do it well. I began to acknowledge I was living a life with many activities interspersed with activities full of self-deception to make it easier to rationalize my behavior. I began to understand that I had figured out ways to manipulate my environment to stay on the left side of the matrix by asking for feedback from those who would tell me what I wanted to hear and allow me to remain comfortable but stagnant.

What causes me pause today is to think that I thought I had all the answers in 1991. The steps I've tried to follow have allowed me to try and get out of the way of myself—out of the way of my high-need-for-achievement tendency to be myopically busy and closed off to anything but accomplishing my own agenda. I thought over time that I would find it easier and easier to go to the lower right quadrant, but it still requires a leap of faith. At the same time, I have become more aware and confident through my willingness to let go of all the answers and follow the steps necessary to try and fly without a net.

No doubt, other writers, speakers, and thought leaders have discussed these steps, perhaps using different language from mine. No doubt, these individuals have suggested other ways of using them to lead more effective, productive lives and careers. Nonetheless, this is what I've found has worked for me as well as other ambitious, driven professionals. I've boiled the suggestions contained in this book into six steps that may facilitate the practical application of it:

1. Stop to reflect, with self-awareness.

2. Let go of the past.

3. Create a vision or specific goal with an agenda.

4. Seek support through mentors and a network.

5. Don't blink.

6. Take action that makes you vulnerable.

These six steps create the probability that you will not be controlled by your fears. It means that as you begin a new behavior, begin a new relationship, take on a new job, or start on a challenging new assignment, you have the capability to avoid or escape the traps of blame, comparing, busyness, and worry and take the steps towards where you want to be. Don't forget that first step, though, as you go on your journey. You must feel self-conscious in order to take this journey, to the point of asking yourself why you are experiencing what you are experiencing routinely. Because if you are self-aware and through this self-awareness recognize that you won't die in the process of doing something new, you keep moving through vulnerable states, your courage increases, and you get closer to experiencing something different. And all of a sudden you find yourself in the lower right quadrant moving vertically to the upper right quadrant.

The journey from the lower right quadrant to doing the right thing well can be arduous, but it will be nothing in comparison with the journey just taken. Not even close. In fact, once you get over yourself and realize that you won't die in the lower right space, the journey north can be exhilarating—full of learning. And then you find yourself in a virtuous cycle rather than a vicious downward spiral. You find yourself on your way to mastery. You then have the challenge to balance the hard-earned knowledge, skills, and behavior change that, if you don't play your cards right, can eventually turn into arrogance.

That is why expressing gratitude is so important at this point. It makes you realize that you are where you are because of not only your efforts but because of so many other factors, namely the efforts of others, the right circumstances, and perhaps even a little luck. Taking credit for what you accomplish is fine as you catch your breath, but don't linger in self-congratulation too long. Find others to thank. To that end, make it a habit to do the following after achieving a goal of any significance:

- Identify the individuals who made contributions to achievement of the goal.

- Express your gratitude to them in specific, heartfelt terms for what they contributed.

- Reflect on all those individuals and other factors that contributed to your (and your group's) success beyond what you did; make sure you internalize the sense of gratitude.

Expressed gratitude and private humility are useful in keeping you moving from the upper left to lower right quadrants and then up to the upper right quadrant—the doing-the-right-thing-well zone.

A Word of Advice, a Word of Caution

I would be remiss at this point if I didn't point out that because you're a high-need-for-achievement person, you're going to have both an advantage and a disadvantage when it comes to the advice I've offered here. The advantage is that you have a gift for accomplishment, and you should use it in ways that serve your need and others' to change. This may sound obvious but, in truth, you're going to find that it's much easier to give lip service to change than to do something about it. Lois, for instance, was a highly ambitious, highly successful vice president with a *Fortune* 500 company who had been told both by her boss and by her executive coach that she needed to become more flexible and a better communicator if she wanted to move any higher in the organization. Despite this clear message, however, Lois persisted in her inflexible, closed-off behaviors. Though she knew she needed to change, she found it easier to tell others as well as herself that she *intended* to do things differently rather than make real changes. She was great at getting things done when the tasks were familiar and the results were predictable—this satisfied her need for achievement. Lois, though, had difficulty seeing how attempting to change her behaviors might result in achievement—it was a much more indirect process and therefore not as satisfying in the short term.

Don't be like Lois. Instead, capitalize on your task orientation and focus on creating specific tasks that bring about the change you wish to achieve. If you want to spend more time being a better communicator or becoming a global leader or working more effectively within team settings, then the way to achieve it is to make a task out of it. You're adept at creating a process to achieve goals, so lay out a process for yourself that consists of a series of tasks and a timetable for executing them.

Because you're so obsessed with achievement, your disadvantage is that you're not very good at expressing gratitude. It's not that you aren't grateful to others, but the happiness that comes with achieving a goal is fleeting for you, and as the happiness dissipates so too does your desire to acknowledge others. You lead your group in accomplishing a significant task, but your reaction is often one of relief rather than real satisfaction.

Rather than bask in the warm glow of satisfaction for a job well done, you are ready to move on to the next assignment or project or

task. The thought of slowing down and experiencing momentary plea-
sure is antithetical to your hyper drive. Therefore, make a conscious
effort to fight this impulse and relish the moment of achievement. Slow
down a bit. You'll have a window in which to express gratitude.

Believing Makes It So

Believing can fuel the journey from the upper left to the lower right
quadrant, or at least it helps us begin on the path. It's important to
believe that this is so. If you believe that the steps I've outlined can
catalyze a change in your work life—can help you not only achieve at a
higher level, but derive greater meaning and satisfaction from it—then
that belief will prove invaluable.

As we reflect, we see with greater clarity the ways in which we
have sought purpose in our lives. We realize the ways that we have
sought identities in what we did, or in the groups with which we affili-
ated, or the jobs we sought out. We grasp the role that status and titles
and recognition played in helping us frame a purpose for being.

Through this reflection, we understand how we tried to achieve
affirmation through being significant or recognized at work. When we
didn't feel significant and we failed to move from the left side of the
quadrant, we found ourselves trying in dysfunctional ways to fulfill
those needs. And the harder we tried, the fewer connections we made
with others because others felt our anxieties and our awkward efforts
to be part of the "club." We focused myopically on doing the wrong
thing well—on working longer and harder but in the same way we had
always done—and we just made the situation worse.

Over time we worried more, and we felt that we were falling further back in the race. As we felt behind, we blamed our parents and
siblings, our bosses and subordinates, our friends and teachers because we didn't achieve what we felt was our due. At some point we

just put our heads down and tried to fill our lives with activities and things and possessions that really didn't make us feel any better. By becoming busier, we succeeded only in feeling more isolated. We felt more misunderstood and out of alignment with friends and families and bosses.

Upon reflection, however, we know that there is a way out. Many have accomplished the journey back toward change and growth. Many have opened up enough to the possibility that old dogs (as well as younger ones) can learn new tricks. This book serves as a reminder that the only sign of life is growth, and it provides a guide for following a growth path. No one has to be doomed to a life controlled by anxieties in which we allow our careers, not to mention our souls, to fade away. Life can be an endless adventure of possibilities. Through self-awareness, with a support network to help us along the way and over the rough patches, with a specific plan, by putting one foot in front of another, you can fly without a net. You can move past the fears and stories of your past that have paralyzed you into inaction. You can rid yourself of the constant internal conversation you have had in the past that froze you in one job, one place, one time.

When my daughter asked me whether I made a difference, I realized later how grateful I was that she had asked. She was genuinely interested when she asked me that question. Shortly thereafter, I realized that in fact I did make a difference in some ways in the lives of others. I also saw that I had spent too much time running from my anxieties in the first half of my life.

The Gift

Mt. Rushmore is a stunning monument. Visit it if you'd like. But you don't need to go there with your daughter to reflect and ask yourself some questions. The fact that you are interested in learning by picking up this book suggests that you are willing to question your assumptions. This may be a first or second step. In fact, ask others to question why you believe and think as you do. Open up to the possibility for reflection, reassessment, and vulnerability. When you are frustrated with someone and you find yourself rushing to judgment, ask yourself, "Why would this person act this way? Might it be something about me as a manager, a leader, or as a person who is responsible in part for this behavior?" When you find yourself frightened to begin the process of change and movement to the lower right quadrant, reflect on the following: "What am I pretending not to know about my role in the situation?" Ask yourself: "What do I think when I see something happening? What story do I tell myself? How do I believe this situation will have an impact on me?"

Reflecting on the contents of this book assists you engage in one form of inquiry that is crucial for change. And in answer to my daughter's question—a question that you may have already asked yourself—I would guess that you already make a difference for others. I would bet on it. Still, I would bet you could make an even greater difference. Perhaps, as you reflect, you might realize as I did that you spend too much time worrying about things that don't serve you well, that make you less satisfied and less courageous.

Know that the adventure to the lower right quadrant will make you feel exposed and self-conscious. But also know that you can't fly without a net unless you experience these emotions, and know that on the other side, growth awaits.

NOTES

Chapter 1

1. David C. McClelland, *Power: The Inner Experience* (New York: Irvington Publishers, 1975).
2. Paul Thompson and Gene Dalton, "Are R&D Organizations Obsolete," *Harvard Business Review*, November–December 1976.
3. John J. Gabarro, *The Dynamics of Taking Charge* (Boston: Harvard Business School Press, 1987).
4. Ibid.

Chapter 3

1. William Butler Yeats, "The Second Coming," http://www.online-literature.com/donne/780/.
2. Viktor E. Frankl, *Man's Search for Meaning: An Introduction to Logotherapy* (Boston: Beacon Press, 1959).
3. Edgar H. Schein, *Matching Individual and Organizational Needs* (Boston: Addison-Wesley, 1978).
4. "The Career Orientations of MBA Alumni: A Multi-Dimensional Model" (Chapter), *New Directions in Human Resource Management,* Ralph Katz (ed.), (M.I.T. Press, October 1981).
5. Thomas J. DeLong, John J. Gabarro, and Robert J. Lees, *When Professionals Have to Lead: A New Model for High Performance* (Boston: Harvard Business School Press, 2007).
6. Michael L. Tushman and Charles A. O'Reilly, *Winning Through Innovation: A Practical Guide to Leading Organizational Change and Renewal* (Boston: Harvard Business School Press, 2002).
7. Chris Argyris, *Knowledge for Action* (San Francisco: Jossey-Bass, 1994).

Chapter 4

1.   Edgar H. Schein, *Career Anchors: Discovering Your Real Values* (San Diego, CA: Jossey-Bass/Pfeiffer, 1990).

Chapter 8

1.   Garrison Keillor, presentation to the Harvard community, Cambridge, MA, fall 2010.

Chapter 9

1.   Personal interview with the author, Boston, MA, June 4, 2010.
2.   Jay W. Lorsch and Thomas J. Tierney, *Aligning the Stars: How to Succeed When Professionals Drive Results* (Boston: Harvard Business School Press, 2002).
3.   John S. Adams, "Inequity in Social Exchange," in *Advances in Experimental Social Psychology*, ed. Leonard Berkowitz (New York: Academic Press, 1965), 267–299.

Chapter 10

1.   Thomas J. DeLong, John J. Gabarro, and Robert J. Lees, *When Professionals Have to Lead: A New Model for High Performance* (Boston: Harvard Business School Press, 2007).

Chapter 11

1.   Paul Thompson and Gene Dalton, "Are R&D Organizations Obsolete," *Harvard Business Review*, November–December 1976.

Chapter 13

1.   Marie Brenner, "The Golden Door's Spa Guru," *Departures*, January–February 2010.

BIBLIOGRAPHY

Adams, John S. "Inequity in Social Exchange." In *Advances in Experimental Social Psychology*, edited by Leonard Berkowitz, 267–299. New York: Academic Press, 1965.

Adler, Paul S., and Clara X. Chen. "Beyond Intrinsic Motivation: On the Nature of Individual Motivation in Large-Scale Collaborative Creativity." September 1, 2009. *Social Science Research Network*, http://ssrn.com/abstract=1471341.

Amabile, Teresa M. "A Model of Creativity and Innovation in Organizations," *Research in Organizational Behavior* 10 (1988): 123–167.

———. "Motivational Synergy: Toward New Conceptualizations of Intrinsic and Extrinsic Motivation in the Workplace," *Human Resource Management Review* 3, no. 3 (1993): 185–201.

———. *Creativity in Context*. Boulder, CO: Westview Press, 1996.

Amabile, Teresa M., Karl G. Hill, Beth A. Hennessey, and Elizabeth M. Tighe. "The Work Preference Inventory: Assessing Intrinsic and Extrinsic Motivational Orientations," *Journal of Personality and Social Psychology* 66, no. 5 (1994): 950–967.

Amabile, Teresa M., and Steve J. Kramer, "What Really Motivates Workers," *Harvard Business Review*, January–February 2010, 88.

Ambrose, Maureen L., and Carol T. Kulik. "Old Friends, New Faces: Motivation Research in the 1990s." *Journal of Management* 25, no. 3 (1999): 231–292.

Argyris, Chris. *Strategy, Change and Defensive Routines*. Boston: Pitman Publishing, 1985.

Bandura, Albert. "Self-Efficacy: Toward a Unifying Theory of Behavioral Change." *Psychological Review* 84, no. 2 (1977): 191–215.

Burton, M. Diane. "Rob Parson at Morgan Stanley (A)." Case 498-054. Boston: Harvard Business School, 1998 (rev. 1998).

———. "Rob Parson at Morgan Stanley (B)." Case 498-055. Boston: Harvard Business School, 1998.

———. "Rob Parson at Morgan Stanley (C)." Case 498-056. Boston: Harvard Business School, 1998 [Rev. 1999].

————. "Rob Parson at Morgan Stanley (C) (Abridged)." Case 498-057. Boston: Harvard Business School, 1998 [Rev. 1999].

————. "Rob Parson at Morgan Stanley (D)." Case 498-058. Boston: Harvard Business School, 1998.

Burton, M. Diane, and Thomas J. DeLong. "Rob Parson at Morgan Stanley (A) through (D) and the Firmwide 360-degree Performance Evaluation Process at Morgan Stanley TN." Teaching Note 400-101. Boston: Harvard Business School, 1998.

Beckhard, Richard. *Organization Development*. Reading, MA: Addison-Wesley Publishing Company, Inc., 1969.

Burger, Jerry M. "Changes in Attributions Over Time: The Ephemeral Fundamental Attribution Error." *Social Cognition* 9, no. 2 (1991): 182–193.

Campbell, Donald J., and Robert D. Pritchard. "Motivation Theory in Industrial and Organizational Psychology." In *Handbook of Industrial and Organizational Psychology*, edited by Marvin D. Dunnette, 63–130. Chicago: Rand McNally, 1976.

Campion, Michael A., David K. Palmer, and James E. Campion. "A Review of Structure in the Selection Interview." *Personnel Psychology* 50, no. 3 (1997): 655–702.

Carlzon, Jan. *Moments of Truth*. Cambridge, MA: Ballinger, 1987.

Chen, Gilad, and Ruth Kanfer. "Toward a Systems Theory of Motivated Behavior in Work Teams." *Research in Organizational Behavior* 27 (2006): 223–267.

Collins, James C. *Good to Great: Why Some Companies Make the Leap . . . and Others Don't*. 1st ed. New York: HarperBusiness, 2001.

Collins, James C., and Jerry I. Porras. *Built To Last: Successful Habits of Visionary Companies*. New York: HarperBusiness, 1994.

Conti, Regina, Teresa M. Amabile, and Sara Pollack. "The Positive Impact of Creative Activity: Effects of Creative Task Engagement and Motivational Focus on College Students' Learning." *Personality and Social Psychology Bulletin* 21 (1995): 1107–1116.

Csikszentmihalyi, Mihaly. *The Evolving Self: a psychology for the third millennium*. 1st ed. New York: Harper Collins Publishing, 1993.

————. *The Feeling of What Happens: Body and Emotion in the Making of Consciousness*. New York: Harcourt Brace, 1999.

————. *Flow: The Psychology of Optimal Experience*. 1st ed. New York: Harper & Row, 1990.

————. *Good Business: Leadership, Flow and the Making of Meaning*. New York: Viking Penguin, 2003.

Damasio, Antonio R. *Descartes' Error: Emotion, Reason, and the Human Brain*. New York: Putnam, 1994.

DeLong, Thomas J., and Michael Kernish. "Alex Montana at ESH Manufacturing Co." Case 405-106. Boston: Harvard Business School, 2006.

DeLong, Thomas J., David L. Ager, and Tejal Mody. "C&S Wholesale Grocers: Self-Managed Teams." Case 404-025. Boston: Harvard Business School, 2003.

DeLong, Thomas J., John J. Gabarro, and Robert J. Lees. *When Professionals Have to Lead: A New Model for High Performance*. Boston: Harvard Business School Press, 2007.

———. "Why Mentoring Matters in a Hypercompetitive World," Special issue on HBS Centennial, *Harvard Business Review*, January 2008.

DeLong, Thomas J., and Ashish Nanda. *Professional Services: Text and Cases*. New York: McGraw-Hill/Irwin, 2003.

DeLong, Thomas J., and Vineeta Vijayaraghavan. "Let's Hear It for B Players." *Harvard Business Review*, June 2003.

———. "SG Cowen: New Recruits" Case 402-028. Boston: Harvard Business School, 2006.

———. "Cirque du Soleil." Case 403-006. Boston: Harvard Business School, 2002.

Depree, Max. *Leadership Is an Art*. New York: Doubleday, 1989.

Dipboye, Robert L. "Threats to the Incremental Validity of Interviewer Judgments." In *The Employment Interview: Theory, Research and Practice*, edited by Robert W. Eder and Gerald R. Ferris, 45-60. Thousand Oaks, CA: Sage Publications, 1989.

Dougherty, Thomas W., Ronald J. Ebert, and John C. Callender. "Policy Capturing in the Employment Interview." *Journal of Applied Psychology* 71, no. 1 (1986): 9–15.

Dougherty, Thomas W., Daniel B. Turban, and John C. Callender. "Confirming First Impressions in the Employment Interview: A Field Study of Interviewer Behavior." *Journal of Applied Psychology* 79, no. 5 (1994): 659–665.

Erez, Miriam. "Culture and Job Design." *Journal of Organizational Behavior* 31, no. 2–3, (2010): 389–400.

Frankl, Viktor E. *Man's Search for Meaning: An Introduction to Logotherapy*. Boston: Beacon Press, 1959.

Gabarro, John J. *The Dynamics of Taking Charge*. Boston: Harvard Business School Press, 1987.

Gagné, Marylène, and Edward L. Deci. "Self-Determination Theory and Work Motivation." *Journal of Organizational Behavior* 26 (2005): 331–362.

Gardner, John. "Personal Renewal." From a speech given to McKinsey Partners, Phoenix, AZ, 1990.

Gaugler, Barbara B., Douglas B. Rosenthal, George C. Thornton, and Cynthia Bentson. "Meta-analysis of Assessment Center Validity." *Journal of Applied Psychology* 72, no. 3 (1987): 493–511.

Gilbert, Daniel Todd. *Stumbling on Happiness*. New York: Alfred A. Knopf, 2006.

Goffee, Rob, and Gareth Jones. *Why Should Anyone Be Led By You? What It Takes to Be an Authentic Leader*. Boston: Harvard Business School Press, 2006.

Goleman, Daniel. *Working with Emotional Intelligence*. 1st ed. New York: Bantam Books, 1998.

Goleman, Daniel, Richard Boyatzis, and Annie McKee. *Primal Leadership: Realizing the Power of Emotional Intelligence*. 1st ed. Boston: Harvard Business School Press, 2002.

Grant, Adam M., and Jihae Shin. "Work Motivation: Directing, Energizing, and Maintaining Research." In *Oxford Handbook of Motivation*, edited by R. M. Ryan. Oxford: Oxford University Press, *forthcoming*.

Groysberg, Boris. *Chasing Stars: The Myth of Talent and Portability of Performance*. Princeton, NJ: Princeton University Press, 2010.

Hackman, J. Richard, and Greg R. Oldham. "Motivation Through the Design of Work: Test of a Theory." *Organizational Behavior and Human Performance* 16 (1976): 250–279.

Heath, Chip. "On the Social Psychology of Agency Relationships: Lay Theories of Motivation Overemphasize Extrinsic Incentives." *Organizational Behavior and Human Decision Processes* 78, no. 1 (1999): 25–62.

Heath, Chip, and Dan Heath. *Switch: How to Change Things When Change Is Hard.* New York: Broadway Books/Random House, 2010.

Heath, Chip, and Sim B. Sitkin. "Big-B Versus Big-O: What Is Organizational About Organizational Behavior?" *Journal of Organizational Behavior* 22, no. 1 (2001): 43–58.

Herzberg, Frederick. *The Motivation to Work.* New York: Wiley, 1959.

Jonas, Eva, Stefan Schulz-Hardt, Dieter Frey, and Norman Thelan. "Confirmation Bias in Sequential Information Search After Preliminary Decisions: An Expansion of Dissonance Theoretical Research on Selective Exposure to Information." *Journal of Personality and Social Psychology* 80, no. 4 (2001): 557–571.

Judge, Timothy A., and Remus Ilies. "Relationship of Personality to Performance Motivation: A Meta-analytic Review." *Journal of Applied Psychology* 87, no. 4 (2002): 797–807.

Kegan, Robert, and Lisa Laskow Lahey. *Immunity to Change: How to Overcome It and Unlock the Potential in Yourself and Your Organization.* 1st ed. Boston: Harvard Business School Publishing, 2009.

Kanfer, Ruth. "Motivation Theory and Industrial and Organizational Psychology." In *Handbook of Industrial and Organizational Psychology,* edited by Marvin D. Dunette and Leaetta M. Hough, 75–130. Palo Alto, CA: Consulting Psychologists Press, 1990.

Kanfer, Ruth, and Phillip L. Ackerman. "Aging, Adult Development, and Work Motivation." *Academy of Management Review* 29, no. 3 (2004): 440–458.

Kao, John J. "Scandinavian Airlines Systems." Case 487-041. Boston: Harvard Business School, 1993.

Katz, Ralph, ed., "The Career Orientations for MBA Alumni: A Multi-Dimensional Model," *New Directions in Human Resource Management.* Boston: MIT Press, 1981.

Kotter, John P., and James L. Heskett. *Corporate Culture and Performance.* New York: The Free Press/Simon & Schuster Inc., 1992.

Kramer, Roderick M., "Harder They Fall," *Harvard Business Review* OnPoint, October 2003.

Latham, Gary P., and Craig C. Pinder. "Work Motivation Theory and Research at the Dawn of the Twenty-First Century." *Annual Review of Psychology* 56, no. 1 (2005): 485–516.

Lawrence, Paul R., and Nitin Nohria. *Driven: How Human Nature Shapes Our Choices.* San Francisco: Jossey-Bass, 2002.

Lindzey, Gardner, and Elliot Aronson, eds. *The Handbook of Social Psychology: Volume II, Special Fields and Applications.* 3rd ed. New York: Random House, 1985.

Litwin, George H., and Robert A. Stringer. *Motivation and Organizational Climate*. Boston: Division of Research, Graduate School of Business Administration, Harvard University, 1968.

Locke, Edwin A., and Gary P. Latham. "What Should We Do About Motivation Theory? Six Recommendations for the Twenty-First Century." *Academy of Management Review* 29, no. 3 (2004): 388–403.

London, Manuel, and Stephen A. Stumpf. *Managing Careers*. The Addison-Wesley Series on Managing Human Resources. Reading, MA: Addison-Wesley Publishing Company, Inc., 1982.

Lorsch, Jay W., and John J. Gabarro. "Cambridge Consulting Group: Bob Anderson." Case 496-023. Boston: Harvard Business School, 1995 (rev. 1996).

Lorsch, Jay W., and Thomas J. Tierney. *Aligning the Stars: How to Succeed When Professionals Drive Results*. Boston: Harvard Business School Press, 2002.

Maccoby, Michael, "Narcissistic Leaders: The Incredible Pros, the Inevitable Cons," *Harvard Business Review* OnPoint Enhanced Edition, January 2001.

McClelland, David C. *Power: The Inner Experience*. New York: Irvington Publishers, 1975.

McClelland, David C., and David H. Burnham. "Power Is the Great Motivator," *Harvard Business Review*, January 2003.

McDaniel, Michael A., Deborah L. Whetzel, Frank L. Schmidt, and Steven D. Maurer. "The Validity of Employment Interviews: A Comprehensive Review and Meta-Analysis." *Journal of Applied Psychology* 79, no. 4 (1994): 599–616.

Morriss, Anne, Robin J. Ely, and Frances X. Frei. "Stop Holding Yourself Back." *Harvard Business Review,* January 2011.

Murphy, Kevin R., Brian E. Cronin, and Anita P. Tam. "Controversy and Consensus Regarding the Use of Cognitive Ability Testing in Organizations." *Journal of Applied Psychology* 88, no. 4 (2003): 660–671.

Nanda, Ashish, and Monet Brewerton. "William Fox." Case HLS 09-27. Boston: Harvard Law School, 2009.

Neeley, Tsedal, and Thomas J. DeLong. "Managing a Global Team: Greg James at Sun Microsystems, Inc. (A)." Case 409-003. Boston: Harvard Business School, 2009.

Perlow, Leslie, and Thomas J. DeLong. "Profiles of the Class of 1976." Case 2-403-087. Boston: Harvard Business School, 2002.

Phillips, Jean M. "Effects of Realistic Job Previews on Multiple Organizational Outcomes: A Meta-Analysis." *Academy of Management Journal* 41, no. 6 (1998): 673–690.

Pulakos, Elaine D., Neal Schmitt, David Whitney, and Matthew Smith. "Individual Differences in Interviewer Ratings: The Impact of Standardization, Consensus Discussion, and Sampling Error on the Validity of a Structured Interview." *Personnel Psychology* 49, no. 1 (1996): 85–102.

Schein, Edgar H. *Organizational Culture and Leadership*. San Francisco: Jossey-Bass, 1985.

———. *Career Anchors: Discovering Your Real Values*. San Diego, CA: Jossey-Bass/Pfeiffer, 1990.

————. *Career Anchors: Matching Individual and Organizational Needs*. Boston: Addison-Wesley, 1978.

Schmidt, Frank L., and John E. Hunter. "Select on Intelligence." In *The Blackwell Handbook of Principles of Organizational Behavior*, edited by Edwin A. Locke, 3–14. Oxford: Blackwell Business, 2000.

————. "The Validity and Utility of Selection Methods in Personnel Psychology: Practical and Theoretical Implications of 85 Years of Research Findings." *Psychological Bulletin* 124, no. 2 (1998): 262–274.

Spreier, Scott W., Mary H. Fontaine, and Ruth L. Malloy. "Leadership Run Amok: The Destructive Potential of Overachievers," *Harvard Business Review* OnPoint, June 2006.

Steel, Piers, and Cornelius J. König. "Integrating Theories of Motivation." *Academy of Management Review* 31, no. 4 (2006): 889–913.

Steers, Richard M., Richard T. Mowday, and Debra L. Shapiro. "The Future of Work Motivation Theory." *Academy of Management Review* 29, no. 3 (2004): 379–387.

Tichy, Noel M., and Mary Anne Devanna. *The Transformational Leader*. New York: John Wiley & Sons, 1986.

Van Maanen, John. "People Processing: Strategies of Organizational Socialization." In *Culture and Related Corporate Realities* by Vijay Sathe, 223–243. Homewood, IL: R.D. Irwin, 1985.

Vroom, Victor H. *Work and Motivation*. New York: Wiley, 1964.

Wademan, Daisy. *Remember Who You Are: Life Stories That Inspire the Heart and Mind*. Boston: Harvard Business School Press, 2004.

Weick, Karl E. *The Social Psychology of Organizing*. New York: McGraw Hill, 1979.

ACKNOWLEDGMENTS

Where to start? While the cover on this book has one name, the cast of characters that made it possible runs into the hundreds. This endeavor is the accumulation of relationships most of all. I've been blessed to have myriad individuals in my life who have had a deep influence on my thoughts, sensibilities, and behavior. These relationships informed me through this rich journey of inquiry.

First is my wife, Vineeta. Her commitment to writing has been an example of excellence in translating thought and feeling to paper. Her ability to convey the human experience through story was one of the catalysts for me to write this book from a more personal viewpoint. Nitin Nohria, my friend and colleague, never left our meetings without pushing me to bring this book to life. His challenges were agitating at times, but they were always grounded in trust and caring. My colleagues Jack Gabarro and Ashish Nanda continually guided me as I observed them teach and analyze organizational change in both large and small systems. David Thomas and Scott Snook asked tough questions along the way.

My agent, Jim Levine, and the team at Harvard Business School Press led by Melinda Merino added momentum and drive to the ideas. Bruce Wexler, a confidant and coach throughout, helped shape and edit this project. Assistant Amie M. Evans worked tirelessly to move the process forward.

I express my gratitude to those research subjects, clients, and participants in courses who had the courage to share from the head and heart. Three specific mentors come to mind who influenced me: Edgar Schein of MIT; Chase Peterson, former President of the University of Utah; and John Mack of Morgan Stanley.

My friend and colleague Paul McKinnon has been an anchor for thirty-five years. He has always connected across time zones and continents to offer support and counsel.

Finally, Sara, Catharine, Joanna, and Jayalakshmi have been and continue to be the finest advisers a father could have. They are each direct, confident in their views, and willing to forgive; I have glimpsed each of them at moments living without a net.

INDEX

ABOUT THE AUTHOR

Thomas J. DeLong is the Philip J. Stomberg Professor of Management Practice in the organizational behavior area at the Harvard Business School. The author of two books on professional service firms, he focuses on drivers of individual and organizational success.

At Harvard, Professor DeLong teaches MBA and executive courses focused on managing human capital, organizational behavior, leadership, and career management. He has served as course head for the required course on Leadership and Organizational Behavior, and has designed MBA courses focusing on managing human capital in high-performance organizations and strategic issues in professional service firms.

Prior to Harvard, he was a managing director and served as chief development officer at Morgan Stanley. He received his doctorate from Purdue University, and his BA and MA at Brigham Young University.

For more information, please visit http://drfd.hbs.edu/fit/public/facultyInfo.do?facInfo=ovr&facId=6445.